Haynes

PC Home
Entertainment
Manual

Published by: Haynes Publishing
Sparkford, Yeovil, Somerset BA22 7JJ
Tel: 01963 442030 Fax: 01963 440001
Int. tel: +44 1963 442030 Fax: +44 1963 440001
E-mail: sales@haynes-manuals.co.uk
Web site: www.haynes.co.uk

British Library Cataloguing in Publication Data:
A catalogue record for this book is available from the British Library

ISBN 1 84425 118 7

Printed in Britain by J. H. Haynes & Co. Ltd., Sparkford

Throughout this book, trademarked names are used. Rather than put a
trademark symbol after every occurrence of a trademarked name, we use
the names in an editorial fashion only, and to the benefit of the trademark
owner, with no intention of infringement of the trademark. Where such
designations appear in this book, they have been printed with initial caps.

Haynes

PC Home
Entertainment
Manual

Kyle MacRae

Contents

Introduction

Home entertainment is a faffy business. That's the technical term. Too many cables, too many connections, too much jargon (see the Glossary for a taster) and, frankly, too much choice. A wander around any 'consumer electronics' store will convince you of that. But what if it was possible to bring everything together in one not-unattractive box? A box that worked with a single remote control, was ridiculously easy to use, hooked up to your television and replaced your hi-fi, video recorder and DVD player at a stroke?

Welcome to the Media Center PC.

Media Center for you?

In this book, we consider first what we actually mean by 'home entertainment'. We then focus squarely on the practical implications of setting up and using a Microsoft Media Center Edition 2004 PC, and conclude with a look at the alternatives.

By way of brief introduction, a Media Center PC is first and foremost a Windows XP computer. That is, you don't lose anything by buying a Media Center rather than a standard PC. However, it includes a special set of add-on tools designed specifically to help you manage and play music, videos, DVDs and, most importantly, watch and record television (and radio).

You can certainly perform many similar functions on any computer, or even build or modify one to suit. We look at doing just this in Part 5. However, we believe that Media Center Edition 2004 is an impressive and broadly successful attempt to bring home entertainment under computer control. Whether you actually want your home entertainment brought under computer control is a different and important question, one that we investigate at the outset.

So… if you are currently in the market for a new computer, and if you like the idea of fulfilling your home entertainment requirements at the same time, and if your home arrangement is congenial to housing a PC in the living room, then a Media Center may make a sensible choice. Perhaps even a compelling one. But does it also warrant serious consideration as a dedicated home entertainment centre in which the monitor, mouse and keyboard are dispensed with almost entirely?

This manual will help you decide.

Copyright concerns

Media Center software allows, even encourages, you to do things that may be illegal under copyright legislation (legislation that is, unhappily, muddled, open to interpretation and subject to local and international implementation). For instance, you can copy any audio CD to the hard disk drive with a single click. You can also record TV programmes and, with a little effort, turn them into DVDs.

True, Microsoft has built in a framework for copy protection measures that could conceivably let content providers embed certain restrictions and rights in media files. For instance, you might find that you can record a broadcast TV show but then only watch it only once or twice before the file becomes unplayable or self-destructs. Or something. The fact is that nobody quite knows how 'Digital Rights Management' measures will pan out.

As things stand, Media Center lets you record and copy multimedia material almost without restriction, and this may technically put you in breach of copyright, perhaps unwittingly. Odd though it sounds, it is technically illegal to copy a CD album that you legitimately own or to 'rip' it into MP3 or WMA files: the

purchase price bought you the right to play the album only in its original format. However, it's fair to say – or at least safe to assume – that content providers are more concerned with illicit distribution than with home recording for strictly personal use. If you record a film from the telly, burn it to DVD and flog copies from a car boot, expect no mercy; but if you simply want to be able to play your CD collection directly from your Media Center PC's hard disk drive, you should be just fine.

PART **1**

So what do we mean by home entertainment?

PART

The concept of home entertainment

'Home entertainment' is a vague term indeed. It means different things to different people at different times and resists rigid definition. Perhaps more accurately, the concept of home entertainment is ever-evolving. What seemed state-of-the art yesterday – remember your first integrated music centre with a turntable, radio tuner and cassette deck all in one box c. 1975? – when briefly rediscovered in the attic, provokes a wry, nostalgic smile before being consigned back to long-term storage. How times have changed, we muse, while wrestling with four remote controls, six SCART cables and a bunch of brushed aluminium boxes stacked under the widescreen telly.

But have they changed for the better?

Digital daze

In one respect at least, namely the ubiquitous advance of digital technology in every realm of entertainment, they have changed absolutely. Vinyl and cassette audio recordings have all but disappeared, save for collectors' corner in eBay, supplanted by the superior and – in principle at least – cheaper medium of digital audio distributed on compact disc or supplied in a popular digital file format like MP3 or WMA.

Video cassette recorders (VCRs) still have a place but digital DVD movies are rapidly taking up ever more shelf-space in rental shops and accounting for a growing proportion of retail sales.

If you subscribe to a satellite, cable or Freeview television service, you're getting digital TV pictures beamed into your living room. In fact, the UK government is still making overly-optimistic noises about shutting off analogue broadcasting altogether in 2010, so one day this may be your only option.

A cheap digital camera lets you photograph anything without using film or paying development costs; and an even cheaper scanner can digitise, save and preserve any paper document or photographic print. You can buy or hire a digital camcorder and make home movies at a broadcast quality level; you can edit your footage digitally on a computer; and you can make your own DVD movies. Even radio is available digitally now, and that's not to mention the internet or video games…

In short, digital technology lets you enjoy television, movies, music and pictures with nary a scratched vinyl disc, an unwound tape or a poorly-tracking VHS cassette to complain about. Of course, now we have other problems to tax us, as we shall see,

So long, to the sound of scratches.

but who truly laments the passing of analogue media?

(Just for the record, I have a good deal of sympathy for die-hard audiophiles who persist in claiming that vinyl recordings sound better than CDs, at least when played on high-end equipment. I happen to agree and still use a turntable occasionally. However, I also happen to prefer the convenience, durability and inherent copy-ability of digital media . . . and I suspect that most of us do.)

Integrated portable hi-fis are all the rage, like music centres before them, and the sound quality can be fantastic. But you'll look in vain for a turntable, and can it play your home-made CDs?

When buying a CD player, portable or otherwise, it pays to make sure it can play MP3 CDs.

Sound . . .

Making a move to the digital age inevitably involves replacing or at least augmenting old equipment with new. It also means keeping up with evolving standards and new technologies. An old music centre or hi-fi won't necessarily have a built-in CD player but you can probably hook up a separate unit to the amplifier via auxiliary audio inputs (if your eyes glaze over at the thought of such things, we sympathise: this manual is very much for you).

You could buy a new hi-fi with an integrated CD player. Thing is, perhaps you did this a couple of years ago but now you have amassed a collection of MP3 files on your computer and you would rather like to hear them through the big speakers. Well, you could use a CD-RW drive to make your own audio CDs and play them on your CD player. Problem solved.

Except that each audio CD can store and play a maximum of 74 minutes of music, whereas a single MP3 CD – that is, a CD containing MP3 tracks in their original file format – could play for ten hours or longer. But does your CD player recognise MP3 discs? If not, it is already semi-obsolete.

You could copy your MP3 files to a portable player and connect that to your hi-fi system, but this is an expensive and rather cumbersome solution. Or you could connect your computer to the hi-fi, but that will require extensive cabling and is, at best, inconvenient unless your PC and stereo system already live in the same room.

Or you could buy a new MP3-capable CD player and connect it to the main unit's amplifier – but can it also play alternative music file formats, like Microsoft-favoured WMA?

Record your own DVDs straight off the TV with a DVD recorder.

A video recorder with a hard disk drive at its heart is not quite a fully-fledged computer but it's getting closer all the time.

Microsoft's vision of integrated home entertainment with a computer (hidden conveniently out of sight!) at the helm.

. . . and vision

It's easy to end up with similar dilemmas across the living room, in Television Corner. Chances are you have a VCR under the TV. But if you're already receiving digital broadcasts, isn't it a shame to record at such a low quality level? You may also have invested in a DVD player, now available free with packets of cornflakes, and the contrast between the playback quality of a rented DVD movie and a video cassette is marked. Wouldn't it be nice, you reason, to be able to record your crisp TV pictures at near-DVD quality?

Well, you can, of course, with a DVD recorder. These devices record programmes directly to blank DVD discs. What a shame they weren't more affordable (or perhaps available at all) when you bought your DVD player. Sure, there are multiple, incompatible DVD recording standards to worry about and blank discs still cost a pretty penny, but a DVD recorder is an infinitely better bet than a VCR. So it's in with the new and off to the skip – or the children's room – with the VCR.

Or . . . why not buy a hard disk drive recorder instead? No need for DVD discs here: programmes simply get saved to the hard disk drive as digital files and can be played back on demand. Of course, free disk space eventually runs out so this raises new questions about how to save your precious recordings.

Forgetting all that for a moment, here's another hurdle. Your TV speakers simply don't do justice to a DVD movie's high-quality surround-sound soundtrack so perhaps it's time to invest in a standalone sound system with a big bass subwoofer and an armful of satellite speakers? What's more, although you may not have appreciated it at the outset, all DVD players/recorders can play standard audio CDs and most also handle MP3 CDs too. At a stroke, a sound system hooked up to a DVD device could bring cinema-style surround sound to your own home and effectively replace your old hi-fi. To the shops!

Or . . . wouldn't it be altogether more sensible to bring your PC into the living room? Sure, it hums and whirs a bit, and crashes occasionally, and you won't be able to work with standard software programs if you use the television as a monitor replacement, and yes, the keyboard and mouse do look a tad ungainly on the fireside rug – but on the upside, it can play CDs, MP3s and DVDs; it can probably output surround sound to a set of speakers; and, with a TV tuner card installed, it can even receive and record television. It also, of course, has a massive hard disk drive for storage, so why bother with CD or DVD discs at all? Just play your media files straight from the hard disk drive.

It has to be tempting.

With budget no object, you could turn your house into a mini-cinema with a 'home theatre' system.

Is convergence king?

There is a prima facie attraction in a 'convergent' approach to home entertainment, by which we mean merging multiple functions within one device. The ultimate goal might be to develop a thoroughly integrated home entertainment system, a one-stop box of tricks, that avoids the expense and complexity of separate devices.

If you're of a certain age, think back to your first music centre and recall the conversation you might have had with your hi-fi nut of a neighbour.

You: 'It does everything!'

Audiophile: 'Hmm. You'd be better off with separates, you know.'

You: 'Better off how? This does everything. It's a self-contained powerhouse!'

Audiophile: 'Maybe so, but you'd get much better quality with a separate amplifier, turntable, cassette deck and radio tuner. And a decent set of speakers. Big ones.'

You: 'Yes, but I'd be broke. That kind of kit costs a fortune. And it's the devil to set up. And it takes up more room. This music centre does everything I need. It even comes with a microphone for making recordings. And a clock with an

illuminated dial! Don't you think the teak veneer surround is rather fetching?'

Audiophile: 'It looks dreadful. It sounds worse.'

You: 'I don't care!'

Skip forward 10-15 years and you could be having the same conversation about your brand new all-in-one midi or mini hi-fi system replete with twin tape decks, 24 graphic equaliser sliders, and flashing LEDs. Skip forward again and you'll find that history is repeating itself.

In fact, there are three quite separate approaches to convergent home entertainment at play here, and it helps to be clear about them right at the outset.

Geek territory

The first is the domain of home cinema (or theatre) enthusiasts, true audiophiles for whom spending upwards of £500 on a CD player, £1,000 on a DVD player, a similar amount for a surround sound speaker system and treble that for a hang-on the-wall plasma TV warrants serious consideration. Specialised, separate components are the order of the day; and the thought of a Windows computer at the controls to muck it all up... well, frankly it beggars belief.

After all, we expect consumer electronics to 'just work'. Wouldn't you be surprised if your DVD player came with a reset

The way we were, perfectly preserved in eBay. What more could you wish for than a music centre in a briefcase?

button or your VCR had to download patches over the internet? What if your stereo refused to boot or your CD player caught a virus? No, keep computer complexity well away from home entertainment, proclaims the separates brigade, even if you need a dozen different devices, a kilometre of cabling, a degree in electronics and a second mortgage to get it up and running.

This manual is not for them.

Halfway house

Secondly, we are increasingly seeing an interesting strategy of convergence being implemented by the consumer electronics manufacturers. For instance, many TVs in the UK now include a digital tuner that can pick up the Freeview broadcasts without the need for an external set-top box. At a stroke, this removes the need for one extra device in the living room and simplifies your life.

Beyond this, though, some TVs now incorporate hard-disk-drive-based video recorders. Suddenly, you no longer need a standalone VCR or even a DVD recorder to 'tape' programmes. A built-in DVD player is a natural extension, or perhaps even a DVD recorder. Why not add a USB port for transferring MP3 files to the TV's hard disk drive and playing them via an on-screen menu? In fact, why not go the whole hog and network the TV to your PC? Add a broadband connection and you could surf the net, too. Before you know it, the TV has the potential to outgrow its traditional role as a relatively dumb display and become the hub of your home entertainment system.

Similarly, games consoles – which are, after all, single-purpose computers – are beginning to ape standard PCs. One to watch is Sony's PSX. When it debuts in the UK, which it should have done by the time you read this, it is expected to include a DVD recorder, a TV tuner, a hard disk drive and broadband internet access. Who knows what the next generation of Microsoft's Xbox will look like?

Or consider the Series 2 TiVo currently on sale in the US: as well as offering hard-disk-drive-based video recording, it can now be networked to display images and play MP3 music stored on a PC.

All of this is happening in a high street store near you now and you could easily give yourself a migraine trying to work out which of the 1,001 configurations suits you best. One central, unifying point is clear, though: the PC as we know it remains out of the picture and out of the living room.

The computer bites back

But the consumer electronics manufacturers don't have it all their own way in the rush to convergence. The dedicated 'home entertainment PC' may be a new approach but it's an obvious one, stemming from a heritage of multi-functionality. Even the humblest computer of the last few years has been able to play DVD movies. True, watching films on a monitor screen is a duff experience but it has always been possible, if not particularly convenient, to connect the computer to the television screen. Every PC can play CDs and copy them, too. Most can make their own. All PCs can store and play video clips and MP3 files. Surround sound is not a problem; nor is television playback and recording, with an optional TV tuner card.

In short, while consumer electronics devices tend towards convergence by drawing upon computer-style technologies like internal hard disk drives, DVD recording and networking, computers are following a parallel but quite distinct path towards dominance in the living room, implementing features that would normally be the preserve of consumer electronics.

Enter the 'Media Center PC'

The Media Center PC is basically the music centre of today. It may not handle hard-disk-drive-based TV recording as elegantly as a TiVo or offer every conceivable zoom, pause and tweak factor during DVD playback – but at least it does both from within a single box. It also manages and displays digital images, copies CDs, plays MP3s and does much, much more.

The Media Center PC is, we feel, a natural evolution. But the drawbacks are, of course, notable.

- PCs are ugly They certainly are, or at least were, but the latest breed are being designed to look just as at home under the TV as perched on a desk.

- PCs are noisy True, but again it's perfectly possible to reduce their background hum to acceptable levels.

- PCs are unstable Yes, they do occasionally crash, hang and stutter. Windows XP has helped in that regard but we have yet to see a crash-proof PC.

- PCs require a monitor, keyboard and mouse Yes, and you'll need all three of these even with a Media Center PC, at least during setup. Thereafter, you can control most (not quite all) Media Center features with the supplied remote control. However, do bear in mind that a home entertainment PC remains a fully-functioning Windows computer. You might well choose to use it to run a word processor, internet access, video editor or whatever else when you're not watching TV or playing music – or, indeed, at the same time.

A TV with a built-in hard disk drive for video recording and Freeview receiver, like this one from Philips, leaves shelves free for other devices. We'd be inclined to add a DVD player but there's no good reason why this too cannot be incorporated within the big box.

A Media Center is a computer-as-integrated-home-entertainment system. And it's not (necessarily) beige.

PART  # A thought experiment

It will help considerably to figure out up-front just what you personally expect from 'home entertainment'. Let's have a look at some of the features that an all-singing, all-dancing digital system can provide. Some you will doubtless regard as essential but others, perhaps, as optional.

Watch television

Odd though it may seem, you don't need a television set to watch TV. All you really need is a TV tuner – that is, circuitry that decodes the signal from your roof-top aerial – and a display unit. With satellite and cable services, you don't even need an aerial but merely a set-top box (STB) and either a satellite dish or a cable feed. The display unit may be a traditional cathode-ray tube (CRT) television set, with or without a flat screen, but equally it could be a liquid-crystal display (LCD) like a computer monitor, or even a plasma screen. Please note that we don't intend to get embroiled in the relative merits of plasma over LCD,

Forty-two inches plus of viewing pleasure to hang on your wall, courtesy of plasma technology.

A widescreen LCD monitor makes a good TV substitute, particularly for confined spaces.

or vice versa, or tackle such supremely dull topics as progressive scan technology, 'anamorphic' displays, projectors and all the rest. That is meat for another manual altogether. Rather, we will work on the assumption that you're happy with your existing television set and merely want to integrate it with the rest of your home entertainment system. To that end, we will show you how to connect the computer to the big screen.

The point is that the circuitry itself is, these days, almost trivial and you can just as easily incorporate a TV tuner in a small external box or an internal expansion card for a computer. In fact, every Media Center PC has an internal tuner card, as we shall see.

If you already have a Freeview or any other set-top box, you can connect it to your Media Center PC and so 'feed' channels directly to the computer.

A couple of complications. There are in fact two different types of TV tuner and you have to be sure to get the right one. Analogue tuners can pick up standard 'terrestrial' broadcasting, which in the UK means only BBC1 and BBC2, ITV, Channel 4 and Channel 5. Digital tuners can pick up 'digital terrestrial

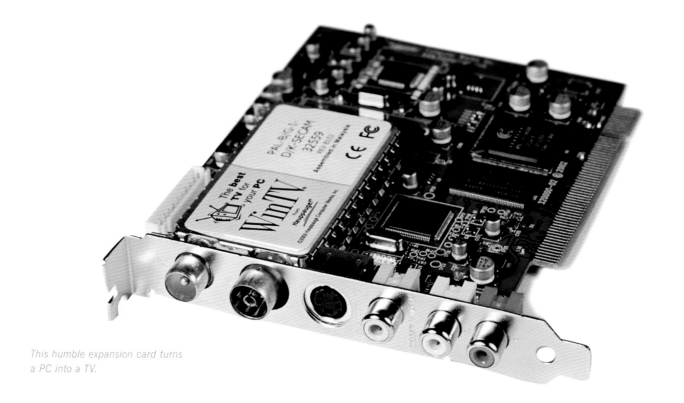

This humble expansion card turns a PC into a TV.

television' (DTT) broadcasts, which in the UK essentially means the Freeview service. This gives you twenty-five digital channels, including the five channels also available on analogue, and a similar number of radio stations. It's also possible to subscribe to a few additional channels for a fee via Top Up TV (**www.topuptv.com**). To see if you live in a Freeview reception area, check your postcode at **www.freeview.co.uk.**

A further complication is what to do with your set-top box if you are a satellite or cable subscriber. What you need is some way of feeding its signal through to the PC. We deal with this in detail later (see pp.39-40).

Incidentally, you need a television licence whatever kind of TV you have, even if only an expansion card for a computer. However, you only need one licence per household regardless of how many TV-capable devices – expansion cards, external tuners, STBs, televisions, video recorders – you possess.

Record television

If you can receive television pictures through a TV tuner installed in a computer, you can also record programmes. Digitally, that is, either to DVD discs or, preferably, direct to the hard disk drive. The days of video tape and VCRs are over.

However, it's also possible to go far beyond the scope of simply recording television programmes. Even a VCR can be programmed to record certain shows at set times, either manually or with the help of VideoPlus codes, so naturally we expect at least the same of our home entertainment system. In fact, we

suggest that any decent home entertainment system should be able to do the following:

- Record any live programme at the touch of a single button
- Schedule future recordings with the help of an accurate, frequently-updated on-screen guide
- Schedule the recording of an entire series in one action e.g. record all episodes of *The Simpsons* automatically and without further question
- Work around 'clashes' where two programmes are broadcast at the same time on different channels
- Work around schedule changes where the broadcaster shuffles programme timings
- Let you fast-forward, rewind, pause and play recorded programmes as easily as playing a DVD movie
- Record a live TV channel while watching a pre-recorded programme (see p.89)
- Provide a choice of recording quality levels to maximise available disk space
- Pause live TV and restart it again when you're ready to continue (time-shifting)
- Rewind live TV (time-shifting again)
- Allow you to archive and share recorded programmes

If you've ever experienced a TiVo or ReplayTV, you know just what we're talking about. Any device that provides all of these features is known as a Personal Video Recorder (PVR).

TiVo was one of the first devices to pair hard disk drive video-recording with advanced features like time-shifting (pausing live TV and catching up later). Shame it didn't catch on in the UK, really, but the Media Center PC offers markedly similar features.

Typical TiVo menus.

Play DVDs and videos

Unequivocal, surely: every home needs a DVD player. As already mentioned, virtually every recent computer has a DVD-ROM drive which, when paired with a software movie player, is all you need to play DVD movies. It used to be the case that extra hardware was required to decode the movie file on the disc – with software alone, playback could be jerky – but more powerful processors mean this is no longer the norm.

A computer drive has an added advantage in being compatible with most recordable DVD formats, which basically means you can throw any home-burned disc at it and expect it to play. The drive will also play any audio CD, and has no trouble with MP3 CDs either. In fact, you could comfortably burn around 70 hours of music in MP3 format onto DVD and get three days' worth of 24-hour playback without any repetition.

However, we want our home entertainment system to play non-DVD video clips as well. For instance, since it's going to be hooked up to your television set, wouldn't it be handy to watch videos downloaded from the internet and saved to the hard disk drive? Or if you have a camcorder, wouldn't you like to see your footage on TV without first having to burn it to DVD? You can also transfer old VHS tapes to your computer and store/play them as digital files. While this doesn't actually improve the quality level, it does at least prevent any further degradation to the source material.

All Media Center PCs have a DVD drive for playing movies and audio CDs

When buying a DVD writer drive or checking the spec of a Media Center PC, look for multi-format support. This model does the lot.

Just like a TiVo, the Sky Plus box uses a hard disk drive to record TV programmes. You still need a separate DVD player to watch rented movies, though, whereas a Media Center has both drive and disk.

Record DVDs

A DVD recorder can record television programmes directly to blank discs using one or more of the recordable DVD formats. These are:

- **DVD-RAM** A DVD-RAM (Random Access Memory) recorder can read data from and record data to the same disc simultaneously. In fact, it behaves just like a hard disk drive in this respect. This is particularly useful if, say, you want to watch a pre-recorded programme stored on the disc while recording live television to the same disc at the same time.

- **DVD-R/RW** This is the 'dash' (or 'minus') family, available in two versions: one-time-only recordable (DVD-R), where a blank disc can be filled once and once only; and rewriteable (DVD-RW), where a disc can be erased and re-recorded time and time again.

- **DVD+R/RW** The 'plus' family, which also comes in recordable and rewriteable variations. The dash and plus formats are not cross-compatible, or at least not completely so: a drive from one camp can usually read a disc from the opposing camp, but it cannot record to it.

However, a hard disk drive is, we believe, a better medium for recording in the first instance. You don't have to fiddle with discs, capacity is seldom an issue (and if you do run out of room, it's

easy to make more by archiving or deleting old recordings), and simultaneous read/write (or play/record) is a given. We have long been fans of hard-disk-drive-based video recorders like TiVo, Replay TV and, latterly, Sky Plus, and given a choice, we would record to hard disk drive over DVD any time.

A secondary consideration is being able to make your own DVD movies from pre-recorded programmes. Let's say you record an entire series of *The Simpsons* on a hard disk drive but the disk is nearly full and there are other shows you want to record. Here, DVD recorders do have an advantage because you simply pop in a fresh disc.

However, a computer with a DVD writer drive installed – that is, a drive that handles not only playback but can also record video on blank discs – can, in principle, copy pre-recorded programmes to DVD at any time. Thus you can make your own *Simpsons* archive when it suits, perhaps even editing out the adverts.

We qualify this somewhat because a) Media Center itself does not (yet) support DVD burning directly, and b) Microsoft has seen fit to devise a modified digital video file format called DVR-MS that restricts, or at least complicates, your ability to copy pre-recorded TV programmes to DVD. However, with a little effort and expense, it is possible to work around these issues. See Appendix 1.

View Song	Old MacDonald	2:19	✓
View Tracks •	Baa Baa Black Sheep	1:28	✓
Shuffle	Three Blind Mice	1:48	✓
Repeat	Five Litle Ducks	1:52	✓
Copy CD	Rub A Dub Dub	0:18	✓
Buy Music	Goosey Goosey Gander	1:57	✓
Visualize	One Man Went To Mow	2:04	✓
	Tom tom The Piper's Son	1:12	✓
▶ 00:06	Little Boy Blue	2:35	✓
Old MacDonald	A Fox Jumped Up	4:15	✓
	1 of 31 ∧ ∨		

Play music

Again, unequivocal. Absolutely any CD or DVD computer drive will play audio CDs and MP3 CDs when appropriate software is in control. Paired with a good surround sound speaker system, top-notch playback is perfectly possible. Alternatively, there's no reason not to feed the sound output from your home entertainment system straight to your hi-fi's amplifier and speakers. Either way, you really don't need a separate CD player.

Of course, when most of your music is stored on a hard disk drive, you won't want to bother with CDs at all. Even MP3 CDs or DVDs seem rather cumbersome when you can play tracks without the use of media. Once music has been copied to a Media Center PC, you can compile your own playlists, mix tracks together, apply special effects and search and categorise music by artist, title or genre. You might even take the time to convert your old vinyl and cassette collection to digital files and add them to the mix.

Moreover, if your MP3 and other music files are currently located on a different computer, there's no need to copy them all across to your home entertainment system: a Media Center PC can play them through a network connection, with or without wires (see p.109).

You don't have to break the law to appreciate the benefits of copying music from CD to hard disk drive. All Media Center PCs let you do this.

Record music CDs

The arrival of a recordable CD format in the late 1990s marked a major turning point in the history of personal computing. Suddenly, anybody with a PC and a CD writer drive could burn their own audio compilations using tracks copied, or 'ripped', from other CDs. The subsequent onslaught of the compressed MP3 file format heralded a global file-sharing gold-rush, a piracy pandemic. Just as suddenly, you could grab a copy of just about any song ever recorded from one of the internet peer-to-peer services, and all for free.

Well, it is arguable that a home entertainment centre can get by without built-in CD recording capability, and it is certainly the case that consumer electronics devices like CD and DVD players do not incorporate it at all. But with a computer at the heart of your system, you're going to get CD recording as a matter of course. We rather like it that way.

A surround sound speaker system designed for PC use but possibly deserving of floor or wall space in your living room.

Surround yourself with sound

Were we so minded, we could fill this manual and another besides with audio talk. But we are very far from being so minded. The only question we're really concerned with here is whether it's worth buying a surround sound system in order to experience DVD movies (and possibly computer games) at their best. If you are not content to pipe movie soundtracks and music through your TV's integrated speakers or the speakers supplied with your computer, you'll need to invest in a separate amplifier and speaker system. Fortunately, the kind of systems designed for computer use translate rather well to the home entertainment environment – insufficient cable length on the satellite speakers is likely to prove the major bugbear – and are generally good value.

The alternative is spending perhaps £2,000 on a state-of-the-art home cinema speaker setup. Which is fine, if you're mad or rich. Frankly, we'd need an ear upgrade to justify that kind of outlay.

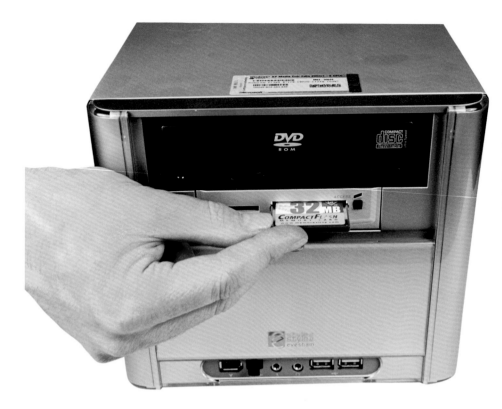

You'll find a memory card reader in just about every Media Center PC. This lets you view your digital snaps without having to connect the camera to the computer.

Display digital images

The trouble with owning a digital camera is that nobody ever gets to see your pictures. Why? Because you never print them out. Why? Because ink and glossy paper cost a fortune. But how about putting on a slideshow on your television screen next time you have a captive audience? Believe us when we tell you that this is far more impressive than it sounds.

Listen to radio

Radio, whether analogue or digital, is an important part of home entertainment. Most cable and satellite services include at least a few free radio stations and a computer's TV tuner card can, when connected to a set-top box feed, capture and record radio just as easily as TV channels.

Some Media Centers come with built-in FM tuners for direct radio reception, although this is not a requirement. FM may seem a little old-hat these days but digital radio, or Digital Audio Broadcasting (DAB), is still relatively new to the UK and we have yet to see a Media Center with an integrated DAB tuner.

However, if the computer is connected to the internet, you can tune in to literally thousands of radio stations from around the world. Fancy a live traffic report for a remote corner of Newfoundland? Just tune right in to the local station.

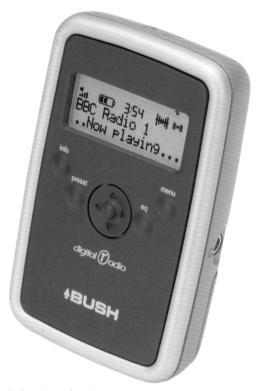

Digital radio has been slow to take off generally and slower still to merit inclusion in computers. For now, you may have to make do with a separate DAB device.

Networking

The whole point of networking is being able to share resources. This is the point to cling to when all seems mired in jargon. A home entertainment system that is networked to a computer in another room can play multimedia files (music, videos, pictures) stored on that remote computer without you first having to copy the files from one machine to the other. The actual physical storage location becomes almost irrelevant.

A networked PC can also, perhaps more importantly, share an existing internet connection. This may be ideal if you already have a broadband line (or even just a telephone point and modem) in your study, as your new domestic home entertainment computer can tap into that connection through a simple home network.

With a home network, you can 'stream' multimedia files from one computer to another. You might, for instance, watch a pre-recorded TV show saved on the Media Center PC in a different room.

Internet access

One to make the consumer electronics camp scoff, we suspect, but that's as may be. An internet connection, particularly an always-on broadband service, is tremendously handy for home entertainment. Indeed, internet access is a prerequisite for a Media Center PC, as this is the means by which it updates television schedules and the on-screen programme guide. The computer itself needn't be hard-wired to a phone line or broadband service so long as you make it part of your home network and share an existing connection, as just discussed.

Play games

Cards on the table time: we reckon computers make lousy games machines. It's not so much that they can't play games but rather the fiddle involved. A mouse and keyboard are useless for most games so you need a joystick or steering wheel or other such bolt-on contraption. You need a souped-up graphics card at the helm, you must make sure that your hardware is compatible with the games developers' requirements – which change all the time – and still you'll experience crashes, blank screens, loss of sound and other frustrations. Our advice is to stick with a dedicated console like a PlayStation or an Xbox. If you choose to ignore that advice, a home entertainment PC will play most games you throw at it – but you'll find no help here with setting it up.

And so . . .

We've just pretty much described a Media Center 2004 Edition PC. This isn't entirely coincidental, of course, as Microsoft set out precisely to address these functions when it developed the Media Center software. Nor does it mean that a Media Center is the only way to tie up multifarious home entertainment requirements in a single box, as we shall see when we consider a DIY approach in Part Five.

For now, though, we'd better take a closer look at this 'Media Center PC' that we've been harping on about.

PART **2** # The Media Center PC explored

PART  Hard and soft options

A Media Center Edition 2004 PC is a Windows XP computer with built-in, bolt-on home entertainment features. These features are controlled by an application, or a program, or an interface, that sits on top of XP and lets you do such things as record TV and play DVDs without having to work with tiny icons or the keyboard and mouse. Essentially, you work with the computer just as you would a consumer electronics device like a DVD player i.e. with a remote control, with ease, and from the couch.

Although you'll soon be used to working with Media Center as if it is the main computer interface, it is in fact merely a subset of Windows XP.

The one thing it is not, however, is an upgrade option. That is, you can't (currently) buy a copy of the Media Center software off the shelf and install it on your own PC. Crazy though it sounds – and it's certainly unfortunate – if you want a Media Center, you have to buy a whole new computer. OK, you may be able to skip the speakers if you already have a sound system, and you might not need a new monitor, but the fact remains that a Media Center PC is an expensive commitment.

Whys and wherefores

The theory is that if you're going to use a computer in your living room, particularly as the hub of your digital home entertainment system, it had better behave more like a consumer electronics device than the average PC. It should start first time, every time, and in general 'just work'. Microsoft figured that the only way to guarantee this was to lay down the law regarding the underlying hardware specification. So long as the computer itself adheres to the specification, the Media Center application should run smoothly and all will be well. Were manufacturers allowed to throw any old disparate hardware into a box and install Media Center software over the top, or were you to upgrade your own computer with a TV tuner card and hope for the best, no such guarantee could be made. Media Center might work fine, but it might not. Microsoft therefore bit the bullet and decreed that the Media Center application would only be shipped with fully compatible PCs.

That does not, however, mean that all Media Center PCs are identical. Far from it, in fact.

Hardware specifications

Here's a run-through of Microsoft's hardware requirements for a Media Center Edition 2004 PC – and an explanation of what it all means.

- **TV tuner** This device, usually an expansion card but potentially an external box connected via USB, 'captures' video and audio signals from a television source. In other words, it receives television. As discussed earlier (p.18-19), there are two possibilities: analogue and digital. Be certain to buy the right one for you. You need an analogue tuner if you normally

This Media Center-friendly video card has three outputs: an either–or choice between analogue and digital monitors (the blue and white sockets respectively) and a parallel S-Video socket that can feed the same video output to a television set.

receive only analogue broadcasts: BBC1 and 2, ITV, Channel 4 and Channel 5. Rather counter-intuitively, you also need an analogue tuner if you have a satellite or cable set-top box. A digital TV tuner is only useful for picking up Freeview broadcasts.

- **Recording TV** The PC must include a software video encoder that's capable of saving a live video stream, such as a TV channel, as a compressed digital video file. Specifically, the encoder must support the high-quality MPEG-2 format used to make DVD movies. You should also have a choice of recording settings, where better settings consume more disk space but look great whereas lower quality settings reduce resolution but let you squeeze many more hours of recorded TV on to the hard disk drive.

- **DVD and CD playback** The PC must be able to play commercial DVD movies, which means it needs a DVD-ROM drive. If a movie is distributed in widescreen format, as is now the norm, the Media Center should display it in the correct aspect ratio. The same drive can also, of course, play CDs.

- **TV-out** It must be possible to hook up the computer to a television set. Moreover, the computer must send the same video signal to a TV and a monitor simultaneously. The idea is that you can switch between office-style work (with a monitor) and home entertainment tasks (with a TV) without having to switch cables.

- **Sound** A Media Center need only provide analogue stereo output but most include a digital output as well, as indeed they should. At the very least, you should be able to connect the sound card's output to your TV set's audio input, thereby playing sound through the TV's speakers.

- **Remote control** The remote should be able to control both a set-top box, usually by means of a stick-on infrared 'blaster' (as we shall see), and the PC.

Microsoft controls the look and functionality of Media Center remotes.

- **Keyboard and mouse** There are no requirements here but we strongly advocate wireless models.
- **Other specifications** A 1.3GHz processor, 256MB of RAM and at least a 60GB hard disk drive are mandatory. Many Media Centers ship with twice those requirements, and most welcome they are too (it's amazing how quickly a hard disk drive fills up with high-resolution digital video files). It must also have Ethernet or Wi-Fi capability for networking, and, supposedly, a modem for internet access (although we have in fact seen modem-less Media Centers).
  You can also expect to find high-speed USB ports for connecting all manner of other devices, including perhaps an additional external hard drive should you find yourself recording more programmes than the PC can store. IEEE 1394 (FireWire) is another must, ideal for digital camcorders. A memory card reader is also pretty much standard equipment. This lets you transfer images (or files) directly from a digital camera's (or portable computer's) removable memory card without having to connect the device itself.

A cordless keyboard and mouse are well worthwhile with Media Center setups, if only to minimise the risk of tripping up toddlers.

And the exceptions...

A Media Center does not have to provide DVD recording so you may or may not get a DVD writer drive. This is an important point if you intend to archive recorded TV programmes to disc, and may justify the expense if offered as an optional extra. However, if you have a DVD writer already installed in a different computer and you network it to your new Media Center, your problem is solved: just transfer the recorded programme from the Media Center PC to the computer with the drive and burn a DVD from there. Actually, it's not quite that simple, as we'll see in Appendix 1, but the principle is sound.

Let's now look at a couple of Media Centers in the flesh, as it were.

PART  Anatomy of a Media Center or three

Although Microsoft lays down the law regarding the minimum hardware specification of any computer designed to run Media Center Edition 2004, plenty is left to the discretion of the manufacturer. Here we lift the lids on a couple of models and sneak a peek around the back of another.

Square fellow

With this model, the manufacturer has attempted to design a Media Center PC that doesn't look out of place tucked under a TV; with a small 'form factor' (i.e. size and shape), it bridges the gap nicely between computer and consumer electronics device. If you were designing a home entertainment PC yourself (as we do in Part 5), we would suggest that this is the approach to follow (as indeed we did). It's amazing what you can pack into a small box.

Note that the top panel slides down to reveal a couple of hidden extras:

DVD drive This is essentially the computer's DVD movie player. In this case, it's a read-only drive that can play DVD discs but not record them. It also, of course, plays audio and data CDs.

Memory card reader Slots for different memory card formats.

On-off switch

Reset switch

IEEE 1394 (FireWire) socket This is conveniently placed on the front of the case to enable easy connection of a digital camcorder.

Optical audio port (SPDIF) This provides a direct line to the sound card's output. A duplicate port is provided on the rear panel.

Headphone port Ideal for listening to music in private without disturbing the room, household or neighbours.

Microphone jack Useful for recording narration while making movies or perhaps even playing karaoke.

USB 2 A pair of fast ports, again front-mounted to save having to scrabble around the back every time you want to connect a device.

Speaker sockets *Used together, these three outputs can drive a 5.1 surround sound system. The top socket carries the two rear channels, the middle socket carries the two front channels, and the bottom socket carries the centre and subwoofer channels. To use simple stereo speakers, either those supplied with the PC or the speakers built into your television, you would use only the top socket.*

Optical audio (SPDIF) *An optical socket for feeding multi-channel sound to a compatible sound system. Wonderfully convenient.*

VGA connector *A built-in connection for a monitor, rendered redundant here by the inclusion of a separate video card (see below).*

Video card *This particular model has three sockets. The blue socket at the top is a standard VGA (Video Graphics Array) style used to connect a CRT or analogue TFT monitor. The white socket at the bottom is the newer DVI (Digital Visual Interface) used exclusively with digital monitors. Between them is a yellow composite video socket (TV-out) for relaying images to a television set.*

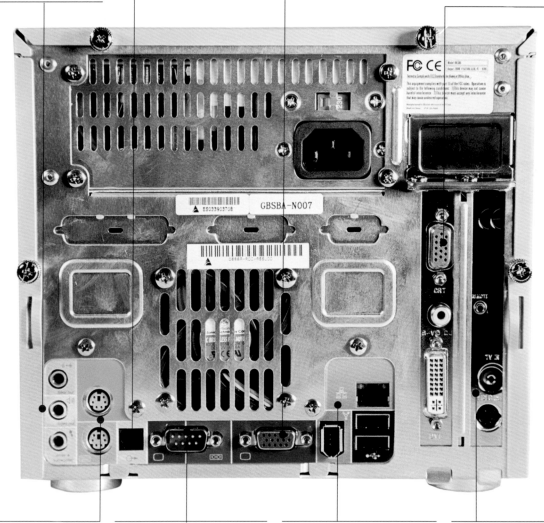

Mouse and keyboard sockets *Must-haves, unfortunately. Here, though, we will shortly be connecting a wireless receiver and using cordless models (p.37).*

Serial port *Old as the hills and pretty useless these days.*

Ethernet port *A built-in interface for connecting the PC to a network.*

IEEE 1394 and USB ports *Alternatives to the front-mounted sockets.*

TV tuner *This is a digital model with a standard aerial connection. This model also has an S-Video socket for accepting feeds from any device capable of outputting video through the S-Video interface, including a cable, satellite or Freeview set-top box.*

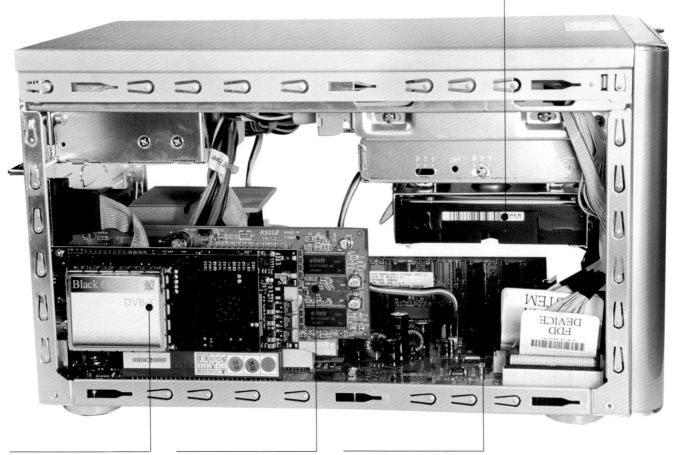

Hard drive *An 80GB whopper, although by no means as large as some. You'll need all that capacity for storing recorded TV programmes.*

TV tuner *Installed in the sole PCI slot (no room for expansion here).*

Video card *Installed in the AGP slot.*

Memory *This PC has one module in place but with room for another.*

Tall guy

In this first-generation Media Center, the manufacturer has gone some way towards living room aesthetics – drives are concealed behind flip-down covers; it's white rather than beige (although the merits of this are debatable) – but this remains a standard-issue tower PC.

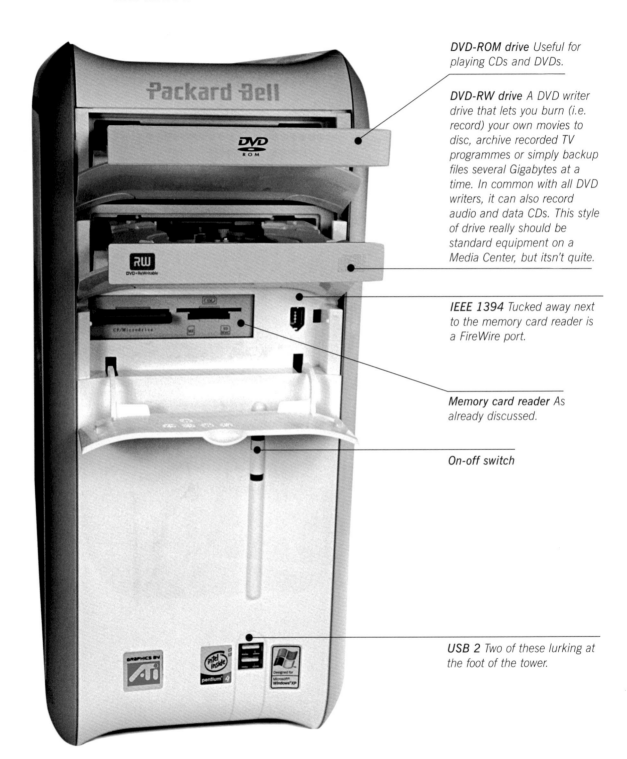

DVD-ROM drive *Useful for playing CDs and DVDs.*

DVD-RW drive *A DVD writer drive that lets you burn (i.e. record) your own movies to disc, archive recorded TV programmes or simply backup files several Gigabytes at a time. In common with all DVD writers, it can also record audio and data CDs. This style of drive really should be standard equipment on a Media Center, but itsn't quite.*

IEEE 1394 *Tucked away next to the memory card reader is a FireWire port.*

Memory card reader *As already discussed.*

On-off switch

USB 2 *Two of these lurking at the foot of the tower.*

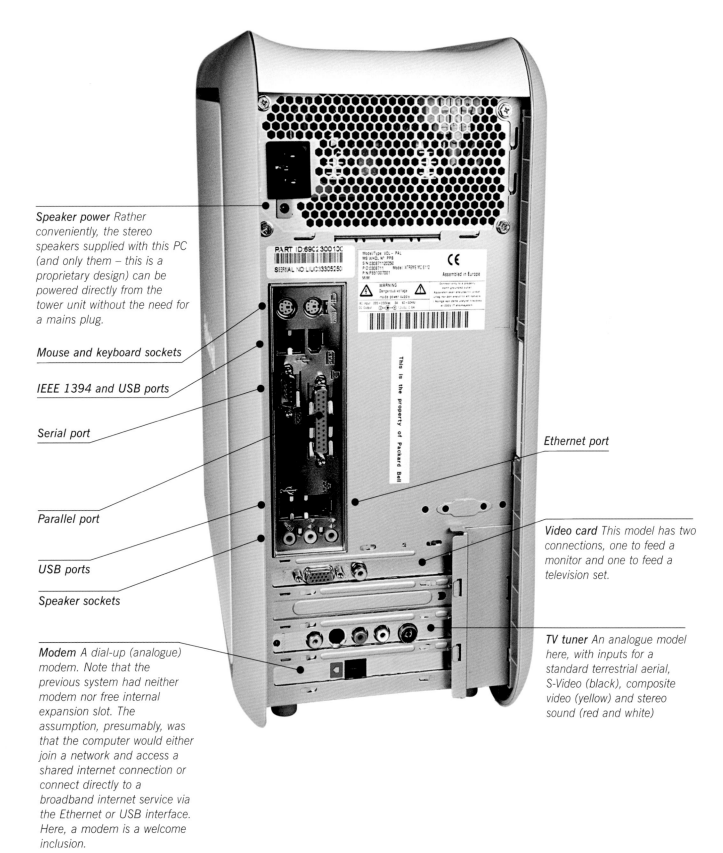

Speaker power *Rather conveniently, the stereo speakers supplied with this PC (and only them – this is a proprietary design) can be powered directly from the tower unit without the need for a mains plug.*

Mouse and keyboard sockets

IEEE 1394 and USB ports

Serial port

Parallel port

USB ports

Speaker sockets

Modem *A dial-up (analogue) modem. Note that the previous system had neither modem nor free internal expansion slot. The assumption, presumably, was that the computer would either join a network and access a shared internet connection or connect directly to a broadband internet service via the Ethernet or USB interface. Here, a modem is a welcome inclusion.*

Ethernet port

Video card *This model has two connections, one to feed a monitor and one to feed a television set.*

TV tuner *An analogue model here, with inputs for a standard terrestrial aerial, S-Video (black), composite video (yellow) and stereo sound (red and white)*

Compare these innards with those we looked at a minute ago. The bottom line is that even with the extra drive, there is a great deal of fresh air in here. Yes, there is room for expansion, but the payback is a considerably bulkier box to locate somewhere near your TV.

Honest, I'm a DVD player

Just the briefest glance here at a Media Center that's notable not so much for its sleek, low-rise consumer electronics design, welcome though it may be, nor for the built-in wireless networking, but rather for the inclusion of two SCART sockets around the back. Oh, how we cheer to see such a thing. As we will discover shortly, one of the most irritating aspects of the Media Center in general is figuring out how to hook up the PC to

the TV – something that is at the very heart of the concept yet almost always requires fussing around with adapters. Here, for once, is a computer that can be connected directly to the TV with a standard SCART cable. Should Microsoft care to rewrite the specification handbook some day, may we humbly suggest that a SCART socket should be considered *de rigueur*, at least for the European market.

THE MEDIA CENTER PC EXPLORED

Making connections

Setting up a Media Center PC is a little more complicated than setting up a normal computer, primarily because you'll likely want to connect it to a television set and possibly a sound system. True, you may settle for a monitor display and/or simple stereo speakers, in which case you can skip much of what follows. However, at the very least you'll need to feed a TV signal to your new computer, either from a rooftop aerial or a set-top box, so don't skip too far ahead. You'll also want to connect it to the internet in order to take advantage of the Electronic Program Guide – see pp.57–63 – without which, quite frankly, the Media Center would be a dull plaything.

In the following worked example, we run through a typical setup procedure. Your situation will undoubtedly vary but the principles will hold true.

Connect your keyboard and mouse to the computer first. Here, because we are using cordless kit, there is a hand-sized receiver to attach. This will pick up wireless signals from the keyboard and mouse and relay them to the PC. Remember to activate the connection between receiver and keyboard/mouse when you turn on the computer later. This normally requires pushing a button on each.

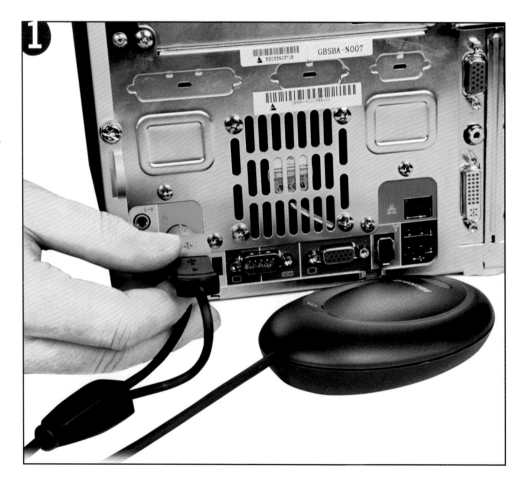

Next, connect a monitor. It's quite possible, likely even, that you'll want to run your Media Center without a monitor. However, while you could theoretically connect it straight to a television and miss out the monitor altogether, you will find it impossibly difficult to complete the setup procedure (we know – we tried). TV screens lack the resolution to display Windows with anything like sufficient clarity, and you'll end up squinting at the screen as you try to configure a network or internet connection. When the computer is up and running, feel free to remove the monitor from the equation; but until then you'll fare far better with a monitor at your disposal.

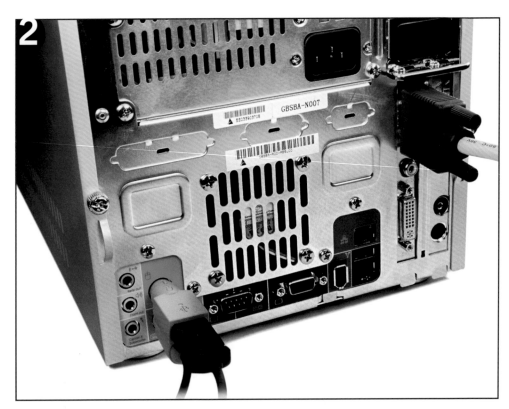

In order for the Media Center remote control to 'talk' to the PC, it requires a wireless receiver (just like the mouse and keyboard, in fact). This is supplied with all Media Center computers. It's a simple USB affair – plug it in and it works – and the only thing you need to remember is to position it so that the remote has a direct line of sight to the receiver. If the receiver slips down behind the PC or TV, your Media Center remote will beam its signals in vain.

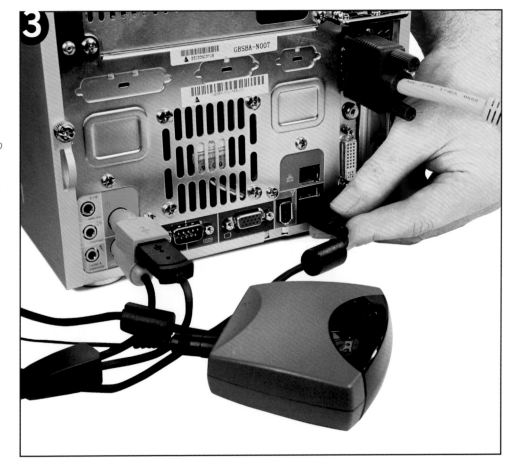

Now think about connecting a television signal to the computer. If your Media Center PC has a digital tuner card, you can run a standard RF aerial cable directly from your aerial socket to the tuner's aerial input. Providing you are in a Freeview reception area, this will pick up and decode all the available digital channels. You won't need a separate Freeview set-top box. If your Media Center has an analogue TV tuner, you have additional choices. If you connect it directly to the aerial socket, the Media Center will receive only the five standard terrestrial channels i.e. BBC 1 and 2, Channels 4 and Five, and ITV.

But if you have a set-top box that provides you with a Freeview, cable or satellite television service, it's possible — and desirable — to connect it to the analogue TV tuner. This way, the Media Center can record all the channels that you normally receive. See p.44 for a schematic overview.

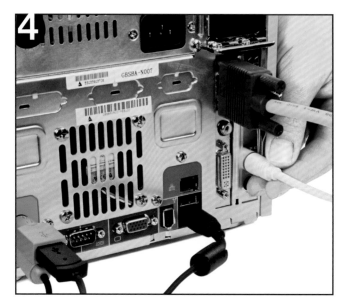

Assuming that your STB is already up and running, it probably connects to your television set via a SCART cable. Unplug this now. Unfortunately, with few exceptions, your Media Center PC is unlikely to have a SCART input so you'll have to hook up the STB with an alternative method. Options are:
• Run a standard RF cable between the STB's output and the tuner card's input. We are not fond of this option. It doesn't always work smoothly and we've seen problems with the sound running out of sync with the pictures.
• If both the STB and the TV tuner card have S-Video sockets, run an S-Video cable between them. Or if they both have composite video sockets, use these instead. You should also connect the STB's audio outputs to the sound card's audio input. This will probably require a dual-phono to single 3.55mm mini-jack adapter cable, as pictured here.

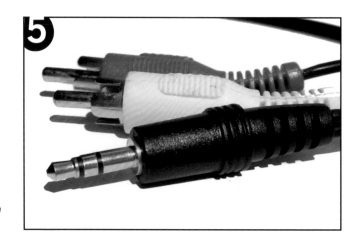

If the STB has neither S-Video nor composite video sockets, use a SCART adapter to convert its SCART output to one of the video formats. The best adapters provide a choice, and also provide phono sockets – usually coloured red and white — so you can hook up the STB to the sound card via the same adapter. Failing that, use the SCART adapter just for the video signal and connect the STB's audio sockets (assuming it has them) directly to the sound card. Again, you'll probably need a phono to mini-jack adapter.

Your Media Center also has to be able to control your STB and change channels as required. This is primarily so that it can tune into the correct channel when you schedule a recording, but also means that you can dispense with the STB's own remote control and use the Media Center's remote instead. The way it does this is with a clunky workaround known as IR (infrared) 'blasting', whereby signals from the Media Center remote are picked up by the computer and forwarded from there to the STB. This is a three-part process. First, you must install the Media Center receiver in order that the computer can pick up commands from the remote, as we did in Step 3. Next you should connect the blaster cable to the receiver. You'll find a socket (or two – it doesn't seem to matter which you use) on the rear of the receiver.

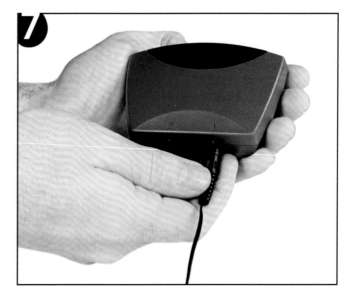

The tricky part. Here you must stick the other end of the IR blaster cable to the STB. But not just to any part of the box – it's important to get as close to the integrated infrared sensor as possible. As this is usually hidden behind a smoked-glass or plastic fascia and of indeterminate size and shape, this is no mean feat. However, a strong torch might help you spot the sensor. Failing that, a little trial and error later (see Step 20 on p.61) will suffice. Peel off the paper from the nodule on the end of the IR blaster cable and stick it in place.

The Media Center is now ready to receive the source television signal, whether this is an analogue or digital feed from an aerial or the output from an STB. However, you can also run a separate cable between the aerial socket and the television set in order to bypass the computer completely. This gives you the option of being able to watch the five analogue channels while the Media Center is busy recording its own input. For instance, while the Media Center is recording the BBC1 from a Freeview STB (or through its own digital tuner card), you can watch BBC2 live on the TV. To achieve this, you need to split the signal and feed it to both the Media Center and the TV set. Be sure to invest in a powered signal splitter like this one; if you opt for a cheaper non-powered model, the strength of the signal will be reduced if you split it once, and degraded further with each subsequent split. Connect the aerial socket to the input socket with a standard RF cable and then use one output to connect to the TV tuner card or STB, and another to connect directly to the TV.

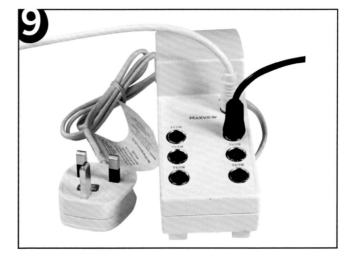

If you want to network your computer, now is the time to make the cable connections. In this example, we are using a wireless (Wi-Fi) USB device. The obvious advantage is that it avoids the necessity to run cables around the house, particularly if your other computer is located in a different room. Given that the Media Center is at home in the living room and a normal PC is usually relegated to the study or a corner of a bedroom, this is quite likely. Networking a Media Center brings two main benefits: being able to access and play digital media (music, video, pictures) stored on a different computer without having to copy across any files; and sharing an existing internet connection. Note that a wireless network is slower and less stable than a wired network and inherently less suited to streaming high-bandwidth video files. Alternatively, if the Media Center will access the internet directly, connect it to the telephone line or broadband service now.

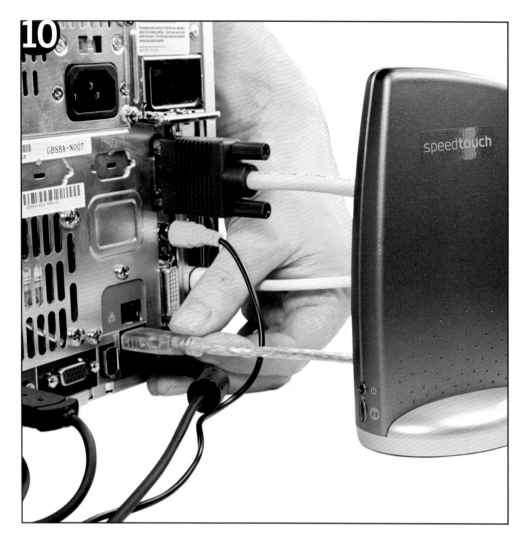

Five words about optical audio: use it if you can. Most Media Centers that we've seen have SPDIF-style optical outputs, in which case a single, thin cable is all you need to connect the sound card to the sound system. This cable can carry any audio output that your computer is capable of producing, from simple stereo to multi-channel surround sound. It can also 'pass through' an encoded DVD soundtrack to an external decoder. Optical audio does, however, presuppose that you have somewhere appropriate to stick the other end of the cable.

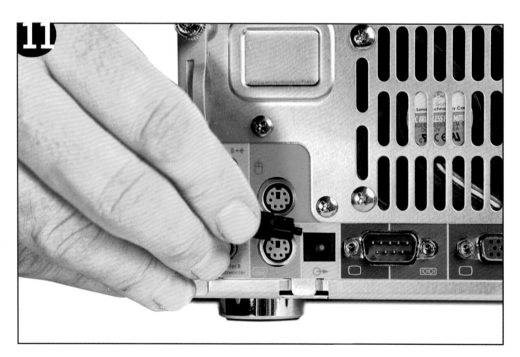

Like this. Here, with everything else stripped to the bones for simplicity, we see an optical cable running from the Media Center to an external decoder/amplifier. No other output is required. This decoder then connects to a subwoofer by means of three stereo audio cables, which are sufficient to carry six-channel 5.1 surround sound. The front, rear and centre satellite speakers would then plug into this subwoofer (or just front speakers if you want a more basic 2.1 audio configuration). However, if you intend to use simple stereo speakers, connect them to the sound card's output in the normal way. Ordinarily, stereo speakers' cables join in a single stereo 3.5mm jack that can be connected directly to a single (usually green) 3.5mm output on the computer.

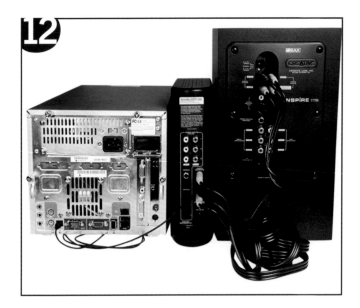

Now for the troublesome business of connecting the computer to your television. If your Media Center has a SCART socket, congratulations: connect it to one of the TV's SCART inputs with a standard SCART socket. If not, take a deep breath. Here are your options:

• If your Media Center's video card has an S-Video output (round, black, with four pins) and your TV has the same style of input, connect one to the other with a standard S-Video cable.

• If your Media Center's video card has a composite output (round, yellow, the same size as an audio phono socket) and your TV has the same input, connect one to the other with a standard composite video cable. That's what we can see in this picture. If you have a choice, use S-Video rather than composite video. The quality is better.

• If your Media Center has an S-Video output but your TV only has a composite video input, or vice versa, use an S-Video-to-composite adapter.

• If your TV has neither S-Video nor composite video inputs, use a SCART adapter.

• If you want to play audio through your TV's speakers, use a stereo 3.5mm-to-dual phono adapter cable and connect the phono plugs to the TV's audio inputs (usually located close to the S-Video or composite video inputs). If your TV doesn't have audio inputs, use – you guessed it – a SCART adapter.

On the opposite page are some connection options shown in detail.

A composite cable connected to the video card. This will feed the same video signal to the TV as to the monitor.

Connected to the TV via S-Video.

Connected to the TV via composite video.

Connected to the TV via S-Video and phono. Here, the Media Center's audio output will play through the TV's speakers.

Connected to the TV via composite video and phono.

Here a SCART adapter is being used to connect an S-Video cable. Note the RF cable relaying a raw aerial signal to the TV, as described in Step 9.

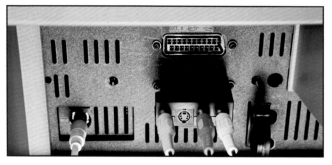

The same SCART adapter being used to connect composite video and phono cables to the TV.

Ultimately, you should end up with something roughly resembling this. Here we see two wireless receivers perched atop the main unit, one for the keyboard and mouse, and one for the Media Center remote control. We have connected a monitor, run a composite video cable from the video card to the TV (out of sight), hooked up speakers, and connected a Wi-Fi unit in readiness for networking the computer. With the final addition of a power cable, it's all systems go.

The big picture

Here for reference is a schematic outline of the main connections. There are several variables, including these:

• A set-top box is entirely optional. If you don't use one, you won't need the 'IR blaster'.

• The signal splitter is only useful for sending a 'raw' aerial signal to the TV.

• Connecting the Media Center PC to a network is optional. Connecting to the internet, however, is required if you want to use the Electronic Programme Guide.

• The PC can connect to a television set using an S-Video or composite video cable, with or without a SCART adapter, through a USB video adapter (see p.128) or, of course, not at all.

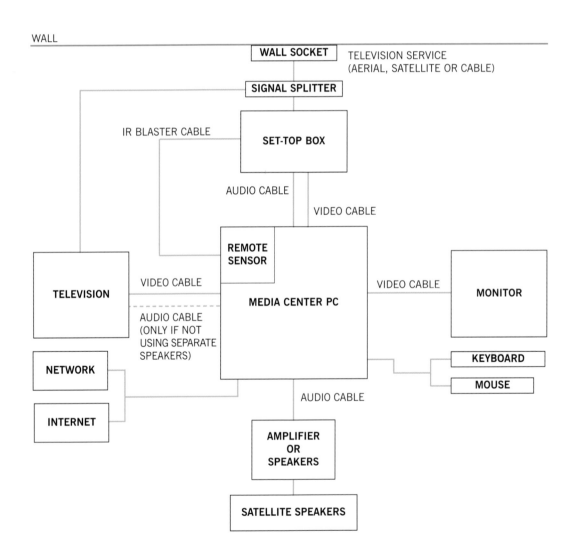

PART  # A little basic computer configuration

Getting started with a Media Center PC is a little more complicated than setting up a 'normal' Windows XP computer, but only a tad. The first main consideration is deciding how and where to position everything. Let's start here.

Four possibilities

The paradox of a Media Center PC is, um, that it's a PC. On one hand, it's designed to be the hub of your home entertainment system, controlled with a remote from the couch and interacted with via the telly; on the other, it's a powerful Windows XP computer that's just crying out to be used for word processing, email, web surfing and the 1,001 other tasks the average desktop machine handles with aplomb. The problem is that a normal television screen has far too low a resolution to display standard Windows applications. Icons are indistinct, menus are illegible, and buttons blur together. The Media Center interface has been specifically designed to look great on a TV – but the moment you have to switch back to Windows XP, as you will on occasion, squinting and eye-strain are the order of the day.

So what to do?

- **Lump it** By which we mean use your Media Center as a home entertainment system pure and simple and forgo all the other stuff. This may suit you fine if you already have a PC set up as an office or family machine and the Media Center is merely a dedicated toy.

- **Upgrade your TV** Either an LCD or a plasma-screen television set will provide ample resolution for running Windows. You can switch between Media Center and Windows at will without requiring a monitor. However, both types of TV are, as we write, ferociously expensive (perhaps prohibitively so).

- **Use an ad hoc monitor** Plugging in a monitor as and when required isn't immediately appealing, particularly if you have

to unplug it from another computer system first and cart it into the living room. True, you'll only have to do this very occasionally if you use the Media Center PC primarily as a home entertainment system, but it's not a viable option if you intend to use the PC as a Windows computer regularly. In which case...

- **Use a dual-purpose setup** As we have mentioned, and as we shall see in practice, the video card in all Media Center PCs can feed a TV and a monitor simultaneously. This effectively means that you can set up a desk with a monitor near the TV set and use the Media Center as both a regular computer and a home entertainment system.

The limiting factor is the cable length. As a rule, monitor cables are relatively short, so you'll have to keep the computer close to the desk. You'll then need to run a composite video or S-Video cable from the video card to the TV, as described in the previous section. There is a risk of signal degradation with really long cables but you should not have a problem with S-Video or composite video cables of up to 10 metres.

Remember that you'll also want to connect the sound card to the TV's audio inputs (if you want sound to play through its integrated speakers), or to a separate sound system, or to the speakers supplied with your Media Center. In the latter two cases, we strongly advise positioning your speakers around the TV rather than the desk, simply because that's where you'll be looking when you use the Media Center for TV and DVD playback. It's disconcerting if the sound emanates from a different location. Again, extension cables are readily available.

Some setups

Here are four possible Media Center configurations in a living room environment.

The simplest of all. Here, the Media Center PC feeds audio to the TV's own speakers so no extra sound system is required. It is not connected to a monitor although, like all Media Centers, it certainly could be on an ad hoc basis. The internet connection (assumed but not shown) is either via a modem or a home network. There's no set-top box because this computer has a digital tuner card.

A little more elaborate. This time, we've included a separate surround sound system for maximum audio quality. We're also using the Wi-Fi gizmo shown on p.41 and so sharing an internet connection over a home network.

Much the same but here we've thrown a set-top box into the mix. It's beginning to look a little cluttered even without the wireless keyboard and mouse shown in the previous two pictures. This, though, is a proper 'home cinema' setup, with a widescreen TV, surround sound, digital broadcasting courtesy of the STB, and DVD, CD and MP3 playback from the Media Center.

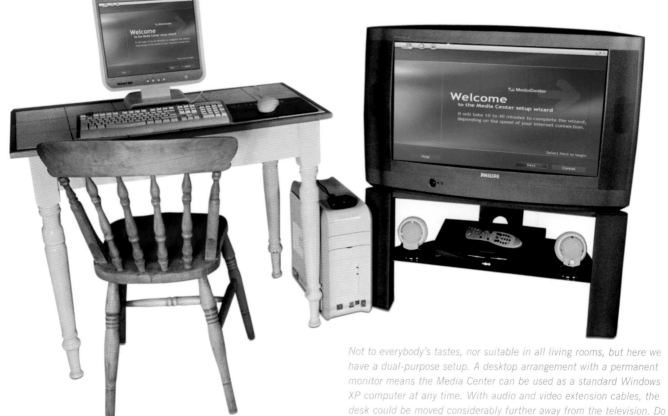

Not to everybody's tastes, nor suitable in all living rooms, but here we have a dual-purpose setup. A desktop arrangement with a permanent monitor means the Media Center can be used as a standard Windows XP computer at any time. With audio and video extension cables, the desk could be moved considerably further away from the television. Do bear in mind that if you're using a set-top box, you'll also need long cables to connect it to the computer's TV tuner.

Video configuration

When you turn on your Media Center PC, it will of course display an image on the attached monitor. However, you also need it to display the same image on the television set, at the same time. With the appropriate PC-to-TV connections already in place, there are two aspects to this.

First, check your video card's settings and ensure that it is configured to output a dual signal. This should be performed within Windows itself, so close or minimise the Media Center interface if it's up and running. Right-click any clear spot on the Windows Desktop, select Properties from the menu, and click on the Settings tab. Now click the Advanced button. What happens next depends on your video card manufacturer, but somewhere in

one of the ensuing screens you will find an option to configure a dual display. All Media Center video cards have the option; the trick is finding it. If you struggle here, check the documentation supplied with the PC. The end result should – indeed, must – be that the TV screen mirrors or 'clones' the monitor display.

Secondly, tune your TV to the channel that relates to the computer's connection (whether through a SCART, S-Video or composite video cable). This will likely be called AV 1 or 2, EXT 1 or 2, S-VHS, S-Video, or perhaps something else entirely. If, like us, you're never quite sure which input relates to which audio-video channel, just use your TV's remote to flip between all possible options. When you stumble upon a mirror image of the monitor's display, stop.

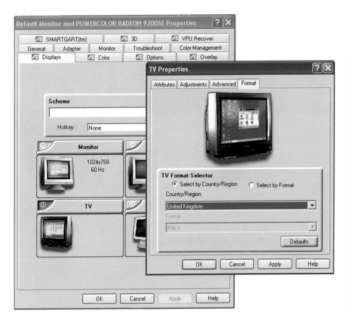

Look for the option that tells the video card to 'clone' the monitor display on a TV screen and check that it's set to the appropriate country or standard (PAL 1 in the UK).

Match the setting here to your living room arrangement.

Audio configuration

A similar but simpler story here: tell the computer what kind of speaker setup you have. Again, these precise options are determined by the make and model of your sound card but you get to them by clicking Start > Control Panel > Sounds, Speech, and Audio Devices > Change the speaker settings > Volume tab > Advanced (in the Speaker settings area). Select the configuration that best matches your speakers. There is no direct entry for using a TV set's own speakers but for that you should just select Desktop stereo speakers.

Network and internet configuration

Just a word on these here. You're going to need an open internet connection when you run the Media Center setup wizard – coming up – so be sure to set this up now. If the PC is connecting directly to the internet via a modem or a broadband service, run the New Connection Wizard (Start > Control Panel > Network and Internet Connections > Set up or change your Internet connection > Connections tab > Set up). If it's going to share an existing internet connection through a home network, run the Network Setup Wizard and enable Internet Connection Sharing (Start > Control Panel > Network and Internet Connections > Set up or change your home or small office network).

A third possibility is that the Media Center will connect directly to the internet but also join a home network, in which case run both wizards and select the appropriate options.

A fourth is that it will have neither internet nor network access, in which case it will function just fine in most regards but you won't be able to use the Electronic Program Guide to schedule TV recordings (or surf the net, send email, download music or videos, stream files from other computers etc.).

Power management

Finally for now, check how and when your Media Center is configured to turn itself off. You can of course shut it down manually in the normal manner from within Windows XP – Start > Turn Off Computer > Turn Off – but it won't then wake up to perform any scheduled programme recordings. That could rapidly prove rather galling. It's also time-consuming and frustrating having to reboot the computer every time you want to watch TV or play a CD.

Instead, get into the habit of leaving your PC more or less permanently switched on. It's designed to be quiet enough not to intrude on your domestic harmony. However, you can let it slip into standby mode automatically after a fixed period of idleness. In this state, it will come to life quickly when you push the main power button on the PC case or wake up of its own accord whenever a scheduled recording is due. It should also spring into action if you push and hold the Standby button on the remote but in our experience this only works if you disable Hibernate mode first. So…

Click Start > Control Panel > Performance and Maintenance > Power Options. In the Hibernate tab, uncheck the enable box and click Apply and OK. Now move to the Power Schemes tab and make your choices.

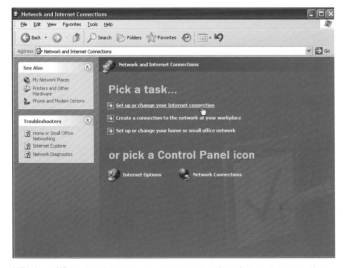

Windows XP makes it easy to set up a network or internet connection.

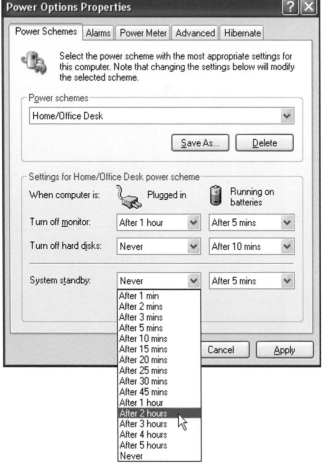

A Media Center PC expects to be left running around the clock but Standby mode saves a little power.

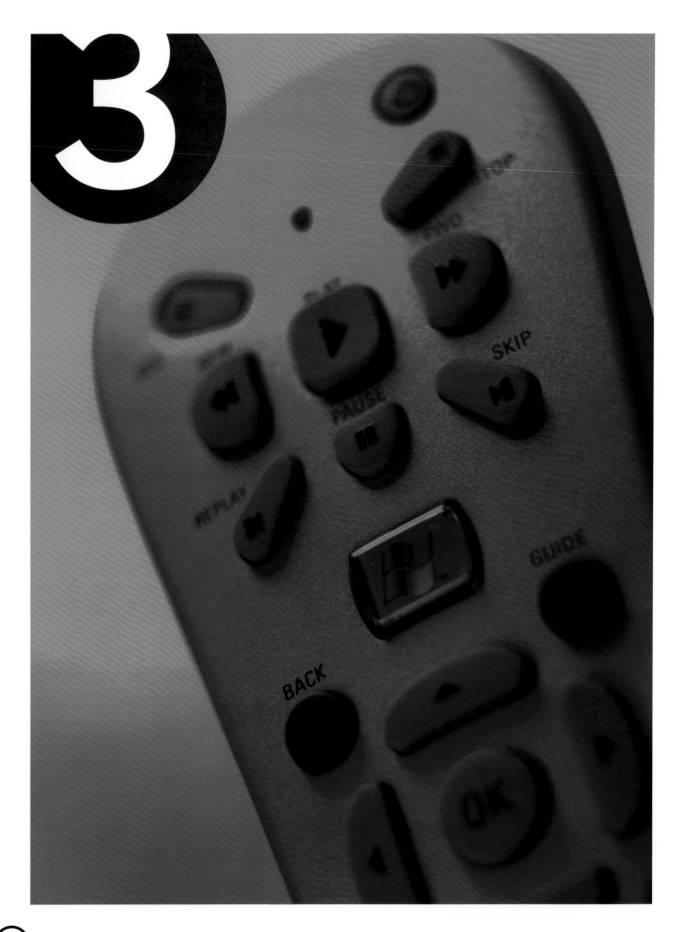

PART  **Getting started with Media Center Edition 2004**

PART ③ The Media Center remote control

The entire Media Center concept hinges on the consumer electronics model of controlling hardware from the other side of the room. This marks quite a break from the traditional role of the PC, and it's hard to underestimate its importance. After all, an entertainment device that regularly has you spread-eagled on the fireside rug haranguing a fluffed-up mouse is unlikely to stay in your living room for very long. You do need a keyboard and mouse to set up your PC in the first place, but thereafter you should be able to control the Media Center functions entirely with the remote.

Here is a cut-out-and-keep guide to the Media Center remote. Just return to this page as often as you need to when first getting underway with your new home entertainment system. Just like any remote control, using this one soon becomes second nature. Better still, it's actually very nicely designed and reasonably intuitive – and when was the last time you thought that about a consumer electronics remote?

Skip *When watching TV/video:* Moves forward 29 seconds when watching a recorded TV programme or video clip, or skips to the next chapter point in a DVD. You can also use this button with buffered TV. Press this button repeatedly to keep skipping forward in 29-second bites (perfect for skipping adverts). Press and hold to skip straight to the end of a video clip, DVD movie or buffer. Like Replay, this button can also be used in conjunction with the Pause button to advance a video one frame at a time. *When playing music:* Moves to the next track on a CD or playlist.

Guide *Immediate access to the Electronic Programme Guide feature.*

Arrow keys *These are used to move around and through options in Media Center menus: up, down, left and right.*

More Info *This provides information (when available) about the current media, be it a live TV programme, a recorded video clip, an audio CD or whatever.*

My Videos *Takes you to the control centre for playing back saved video clips.*

My Pictures *Access to your digital image collection starts here.*

My Music *Audio central. Use this button to prepare to play CDs and saved MP3/WMA tracks.*

My TV *A shortcut to everything pertaining to watching and recording TV programmes.*

Mute *Kill the sound.*

DVD Menu *Hop straight to the title page in a commercial (or self-authored) DVD movie.*

Clear *Clears the last number or letter entered with the number pad.*

Enter *Confirms numbers or text entered with the number pad.*

Playback (or 'transport') controls *These buttons are used to control TV, video and music playback. They work just like you would expect with a couple of important extras. In detail:*

REC *When watching TV/video:* A one-touch button for recording the current live TV programme to the hard disk. *When playing music:* n/a.

Replay *When watching TV/video:* Replays the last 7 seconds of a live or recorded TV programme or video clip, or returns to the previous chapter point in a DVD. This button can be used repeatedly to keep skipping back in 7-second bites. Alternatively, press and hold the button to go straight back to the beginning of a video clip, DVD movie or buffer (see p.77). You can also use the Pause button to freeze the current video frame and then work back one frame at a time. *When playing music:* Replays the last track on a CD or playlist.

Back *Wherever you are in a Media Center menu, this button takes you back one step, page, screen or however you like to think of it. Use repeatedly to backtrack until you find your starting point.*

Live TV *Hide the Media Center interface and go straight to the currently selected TV channel in full-screen mode.*

Volume *Increase or decrease the volume for the current media. Note that you may also have to use your TV or separate sound system's controls to govern overall playback volume.*

Number pad *Use these to enter numbers and/or letters as required in Media Center menus, which is rarely, or to enter channel numbers when watching live TV. If you're familiar with sending text messages on a mobile phone, you'll understand the multi-tap methodology: for example one press on the number 1 button generates a number 1; a second, rapid press generates the letter G; a third equally rapid press generates an H; and so on.*

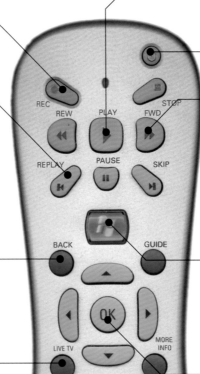

Play, Stop and Pause *When watching TV/video:* Starts, stops and pauses playback of the current video (again, this could be a DVD, clip or recording). The Pause button also works with live television – i.e. it freezes the current programme – which takes some getting used to but will change your viewing habits forever. *When playing music:* Starts, stops and pauses playback of the current track or playlist.

Standby *Turns the Media Center PC on and not-quite off (p.49).*

REW and FWD *When watching TV/video:* Changes direction and speeds up playback of DVD movies, video clips and recorded TV. One press doubles the speed, two presses increases speed by a factor of 40, and three presses bumps this right up to 250x speed. *When playing music:* The FWD button speeds up music playback – one press plays the current track at 1.4x speed, two presses at 5x speed – but the REW button does nothing.

Start *A big green button that launches the Media Center application. It can also be used to skip straight to the main Media Center menu at any time, which is useful if you find yourself several pages deep into a configuration menu and want to return quickly to the main launchpad.*

OK *Think of this as the Enter or Return key on a keyboard. Essentially, it says 'yes' to the current option and activates playback or some other function. If any button will wear out through constant use, this is the one.*

Channel/Page *Change channels up and down. This button can control the television broadcast received directly by the PC or indirectly via a set-top box. We talk about how to set it up on p.61. It also functions as a page-changing button in Media Center menus. When confronted with a list of options that's too long to fit on a single on-screen page, this button scrolls through the list a page at a time. It's basically a faster alternative to the up and down arrow keys.*

PART  The Media Center setup wizard

As is the Windows way, Media Center comes with a useful wizard to get you started. Before running it, ensure that your TV screen is displaying the same image as your monitor and open a live internet connection. You should also have made all the connections discussed earlier, including – most importantly of all – a TV signal input from a set-top box or through a direct aerial connection (analogue or digital). Two additional things you'll need here are your TV's remote control and your post code.

Point your Media Center remote control at the IR receiver and press the big green button. Or, if you prefer, use the mouse to click the Media Center shortcut on the Windows Desktop. This launches the Media Center interface with the setup wizard ready to roll. The familiar Windows XP Desktop should disappear completely behind it. However, if you move the mouse anywhere within the Media Center window, you will see a grey toolbar appear at the top of the Media Center screen. When this is visible, you can resize Media Center to a window rather than full screen, or minimise it to the Taskbar, or close it altogether. In fact, it behaves just like any other program in Windows. Full screen display is simply its default mode.

Restore Media Center to full screen and note how the Next button is currently coloured green. This is Media Center's selection style: when a button is green, it is selected, and it can then be activated (or clicked, if you prefer) by pressing the OK button on the remote control (or the return key on the keyboard). You can also use the left, right, up and down arrows that surround the OK button on the remote to change the on-screen selection around. For instance, one press of the right arrow would highlight the Cancel button. Try this now. When you're comfortable working with the remote, highlight the Next button again and press OK.

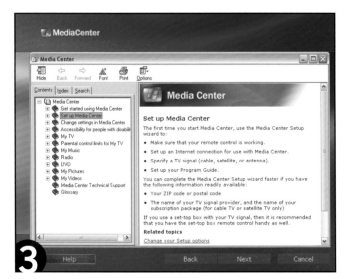

Four processes await your attention and we'll work through these in turn. First, though, that Help button in the bottom-left corner of the Media Center screen. At any time, you can select this with the arrow buttons and press OK to see a Help menu in a separate window. You'll have to read the directions on your monitor screen rather than the TV as the Help menu is not designed with the same large font as the Media Center interface (which is rather a pity). Select Next to continue.

The first procedure couldn't be simpler. Press the numbered buttons on your remote and check that the corresponding numbers highlight on screen. If this doesn't work, press the down arrow to select the 'I'm having problems' option, press OK once to activate it, and press OK again when the Next button is green. Ironically, of course, you won't be able to do any of this if the remote is completely non-functional, so use the mouse instead.

This isn't much of a troubleshooter, to be frank. In virtually every case, the problem will be one of reception, in the sense that the IR sensor is unable to pick up the remote's signal. We're sure that you remembered to put batteries in the remote – check anyway – but do be sure that you're pointing the remote at the computer, not the TV (not quite as silly a suggestion as it sounds). Also check that the sensor is visible. If it's slipped down the back of the PC, the remote may be beaming out its instructions to a blind eye. When you've established a connection, activate the Try again button to return to the previous screen, and select the working properly option (shown in the previous step). Press OK to activate it. The Next button will then highlight, so press OK once more to proceed.

The wizard now invites you to configure your Guide updates over the internet. This is an important step, as without it you will be unable to view current and future TV schedules or take advantage of Media Center's advanced video recording features. If your Media Center is connected to an always-on broadband connection, either directly or through a network, select the default Download when connected option. The computer will then automatically update its Guide without your involvement. If you have a dial-up connection but you're certain that you'll connect at least once a day, you can leave this option selected and hope that Media Center manages to grab the data it needs when the opportunity presents itself. However, we suggest that manual downloads are the way to go with a dial-up internet connection. This way, you must actively request and control your Guide updates (see p.85 for instructions). Make your selection and proceed.

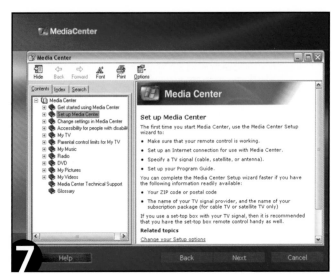

If you opted to download data when connected, the wizard will now give you an opportunity to test the connection. If this is successful, proceed. If not, as shown here, you need to get to the root of the problem. However, this is not a task for Media Center. Rather, minimise the Media Center interface (see Step 1) and return to a standard Windows environment. Work through all the usual options in Network Connections, accessed through the Control Panel, and get your direct or shared internet connection working properly. Visit a few web pages to be sure. Return to this screen and try again. So long as there is an open line to the internet, Media Center should find it and confirm that all is well.

However, it's possible that the wizard will stumble at this point even when the computer is definitely connected to the internet. The best bet is to close Media Center (but leave the Run Wizard next time I start Media Center option selected). With your internet connection still alive, restart Media Center – use the green button on the remote – and proceed through Steps 1-7 again. If you still have no luck, close Media Center and restart the computer. Re-establish the internet connection, relaunch Media Center and run through the wizard once more. This time, you should certainly succeed. Select Next to continue.

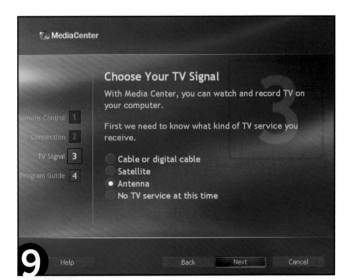

It's time to tell Media Center about your television service. In this example, we're using a Freeview set-top box connected to an analogue TV tuner card, so the correct selection is Antenna. That is, our television pictures are received through an aerial rather than a satellite or cable service. If you have a digital TV tuner card, you should also select Antenna. If you have a satellite or cable STB connected to your Media Center, make the appropriate selection.

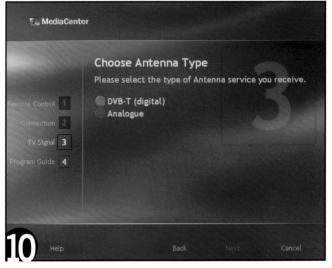

Here we must tell Media Center whether we receive analogue-only channels or a digital service. Note that Freeview usually goes by the name of DTT, or Digital Terrestrial Television, whereas here the option is listed as DVB-T, or Digital Video Broadcast - Terrestrial. They mean the same thing. If you currently get Freeview through a set-top box, or if your Media Center has a digital TV tuner card, select DVB-T here. Otherwise, select Analogue.

In this step, select No only if you have a digital TV tuner in your Media Center or if the computer has an analogue card but is connected directly to the RF aerial socket. In all other cases, whether you have a Freeview, cable or satellite set-top box, select Yes. The next screen (not shown) asks to ensure that your STB is turned on; that you've made all the proper connections between the STB, your PC and the TV; and, vitally, that the IR control cable is stuck in position (see p.40). These conditions all being met, click Next once more to proceed to the testing phase.

The option you must select in this ill-designed and confusing screen is determined by the manner in which your STB is connected to your computer's TV tuner card. We recommend using the mouse and keyboard rather than the remote to make selections here. Select the top option if you're using an RF aerial cable, the second if you're using an S-Video cable (with or without a SCART adapter) and the third if you have a composite video connection. The idea is to get a television picture displaying in the box. So long as your STB box is tuned to a channel, this should be automatic.

In our experience, however, it isn't always so. The problematic setting tends to be the top one, corresponding to a simple RF aerial connection. Use the keyboard to enter a channel number and hit return. If you don't see anything, try another channel number and hit return again. Quite what this channel hopping does, we have no idea – and Media Center doesn't explain. In any case, don't proceed – i.e. don't click Next – until you see something in the video box, even if it's only static.

In this shot, we have selected the Composite Video option and been rewarded with a nice, clear television picture. This is because the set-top box is connected to the computer by means of a composite video cable, one of the options described on pp.42–43. It's well worthwhile testing your audio signal at this point, incidentally: switch on your speakers and make sure that you can hear the programme as well as see it.

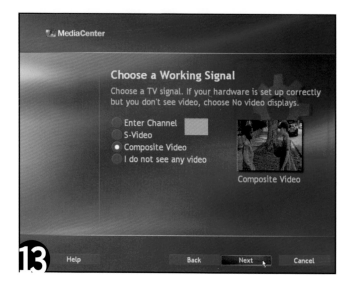

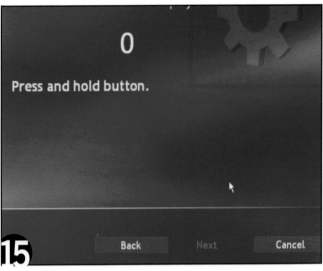

These next few steps are relatively straightforward so we'll hurry through them. Here, select Yes – you do have a remote for your STB, presumably – and click Next. The ensuing screen asks you to prepare the remote by ensuring it is set up to correctly control TV channels. This is only really an issue for multi-function or 'universal' remotes that learn how to control several devices, including TVs, hi-fis, DVD players and the like, and can be switched from one mode to another.

Follow the instructions and cross your fingers that Media Center can identify your set-top box's remote control. Essentially, the Media Center's sensor compares the remote's coded signal against a known database. If it finds a match, you should be able to control the STB directly with the Media Center remote.

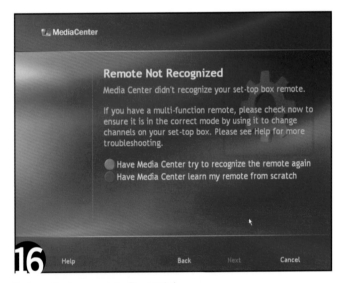

It doesn't always work. Try again!

That's better. Select Next to continue.

18 Self-explanatory, although you do need to know the answer. With Freeview, the correct answer is three digits.

19 Again, fairly obvious. Most remotes change channels as soon as you tap in the number but a few require additional confirmation.

An interesting juncture. The wizard now invites you to use the Media Center's own remote control to change channels on the set-top box. This is when you learn whether the previous few steps have been successful. Use the number pad to tap in a channel number that you can definitely receive exactly as you would with the STB's remote. Here, because we're using Freeview, we tried 40, which corresponds to the BBC News 24 channel. Your STB should change channel accordingly, and you should see the correct channel displayed in the video box. If not, try adjusting the position of the stick-on IR 'blaster' on the STB fascia (see p.40).

When it works, select the 'channel changed correctly' option and proceed (or tell Media Center that the test failed and work through the previous steps again). Incidentally, you can't use the mouse to select the options here, so revert to the remote. That is, use the up and down arrows as necessary to highlight 'The channel changed correctly', press OK to select it, wait for the Next button to become highlighted, and press OK again to proceed.

20

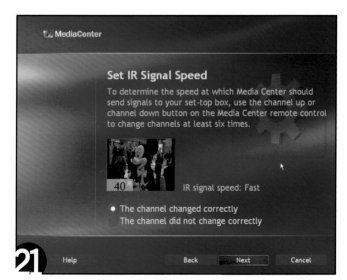

Set IR Signal Speed

To determine the speed at which Media Center should send signals to your set-top box, use the channel up or channel down button on the Media Center remote control to change channels at least six times.

40

IR signal speed: Fast

● The channel changed correctly
○ The channel did not change correctly

21 Help | Back | Next | Cancel

Now you must indulge in a little channel hopping with the Media Center remote's Channel/Page button. You'll probably suffer a small but significant delay between pressing the button and the channel changing but that's just the nature of the IR 'blaster' beast. This step seeks to find the best possible compromise. Proceed only when the channels change correctly each time.

Protecting your Privacy

Microsoft is committed to protecting your privacy. The next few screens will allow you to control some important Media Center features that collect or share information.

For more information about Media Center and your privacy, please read our privacy statement.

View the Media Center privacy statement

Remote Control 1
Connection 2
TV Signal 3
Program Guide 4

22 Help | Back | Next | Cancel

We're now moving into the final stage of the setup wizard, and this is arguably the most important bit of all. As we've mentioned, Media Center comes with an Electronic Program Guide. This is a detailed 14-day TV guide customised to your particular region and television service. We'll be working with it in detail shortly but now we have to get it up and running. Before going any further, just check that your internet connection is still open. Then read the privacy statement provided here and click Next to proceed.

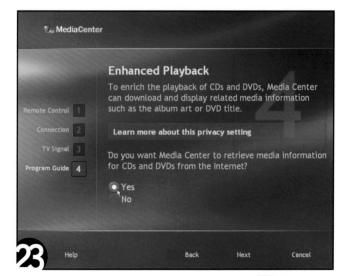

Enhanced Playback

To enrich the playback of CDs and DVDs, Media Center can download and display related media information such as the album art or DVD title.

Learn more about this privacy setting

Do you want Media Center to retrieve media information for CDs and DVDs from the Internet?

● Yes
○ No

Remote Control 1
Connection 2
TV Signal 3
Program Guide 4

23 Help | Back | Next | Cancel

We suggest selecting Yes here and allowing Media Center to retrieve media information from the internet. This can make working with ripped CDs and rented movies a little more rewarding later. However, it's optional. If you have any doubts, check that you're happy with the privacy statement.

Program Guide

The Guide provides TV listings to help you find, watch, and record TV shows. If you use the Guide, anonymous information to improve the quality and accuracy of the service will be sent to Microsoft.

View the Guide privacy statement

Do you want to use the Guide?

● Yes
○ No

Remote Control 1
Connection 2
TV Signal 3
Program Guide 4

24 Help | Back | Next | Cancel

This really is a no-brainer: if you don't use the Guide, your Media Center won't function as a proper Personal Video Recorder (see p.19). Select Yes and continue. The following screen provides 31 pages of legalese. Select I agree, and press Next to continue.

If you can figure out how to make the Media Center remote enter the letters required for UK post codes, do please share the secret: mobile phone-style multi-tapping doesn't seem to work on this screen. So, revert to the keyboard and type in your details. When you click Next, Media Center connects to the Guide service on the internet and attempts to identify your TV service provider, based on your earlier responses. This may take a few minutes. Click Next again when invited to continue.

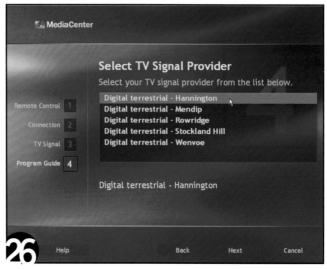

*Rather awkwardly, you may now have to select your nearest (or strongest) terrestrial television signal. If you're using Freeview, check **www.freeview.co.uk** for details. Otherwise, be prepared to return here and experiment. Make your selection and click Next.*

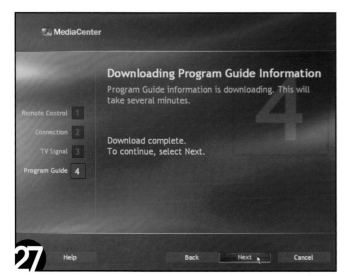

Media Center now downloads full television listings for all channels that are available to you. This will certainly take a while, even over broadband. Be patient; it's almost exciting! When the download is complete, click Next.

At last, the wizard comes to a close and you can click Finish. Doing so takes you to the main Media Center menu.

PART  # A few final settings

Before getting to grips with the various modules in Media Center Edition 2004, it pays to check that everything is set up to best effect.

On screen now should be the main Media Center menu with a list of options: Play DVD, My Pictures, My TV and so forth. At this point, you can dispense with monitor, mouse and keyboard altogether if you so choose, and work entirely with the Media Center remote. However, we recommend keeping at least the mouse to hand for now.

We'd also suggest that now is a good time to set up Windows Media Player. This is a multimedia file player supplied with Windows XP and it underpins several Media Center features. However, it can only be modified from a Windows environment, not from within Media Center itself, and requires a keyboard and mouse. Configuration directions are given on pp.98–102.

Menu antics

Try scrolling through the onscreen menu using the arrow keys on your Media Center remote control. When you press the down arrow once, the next item in the list becomes highlighted. Pressing the OK button would take you to that module. Press the down arrow again to keep stepping through the list. In fact, this menu is circular so if you keep pressing the down arrow you'll eventually get back to your starting point. You can scroll with the up arrow as well, needless to say.

The left and right arrows, meanwhile, take you to different areas of the menu. See if you can get to the minimise, restore down (i.e. windowed-mode) and close buttons in the top-right corner. As we saw earlier, you can summon an additional toolbar with copies of these buttons by moving the mouse anywhere within the Media Center interface, but now you should practice working with just the remote.

When the middle button is highlighted, press OK. Media Center will reduce in size to a window on the Windows XP Desktop.

The same button will remain highlighted and a further press on OK restores Media Center to full screen. You can change the size of the Media Center window and/or reposition it on the Desktop, but only by dragging it in or out with the mouse, not via the remote. Media Center remembers where you leave the window and always snaps into the same size and position next time you invoke windowed mode. Return to the module list by pressing the left arrow a couple of times.

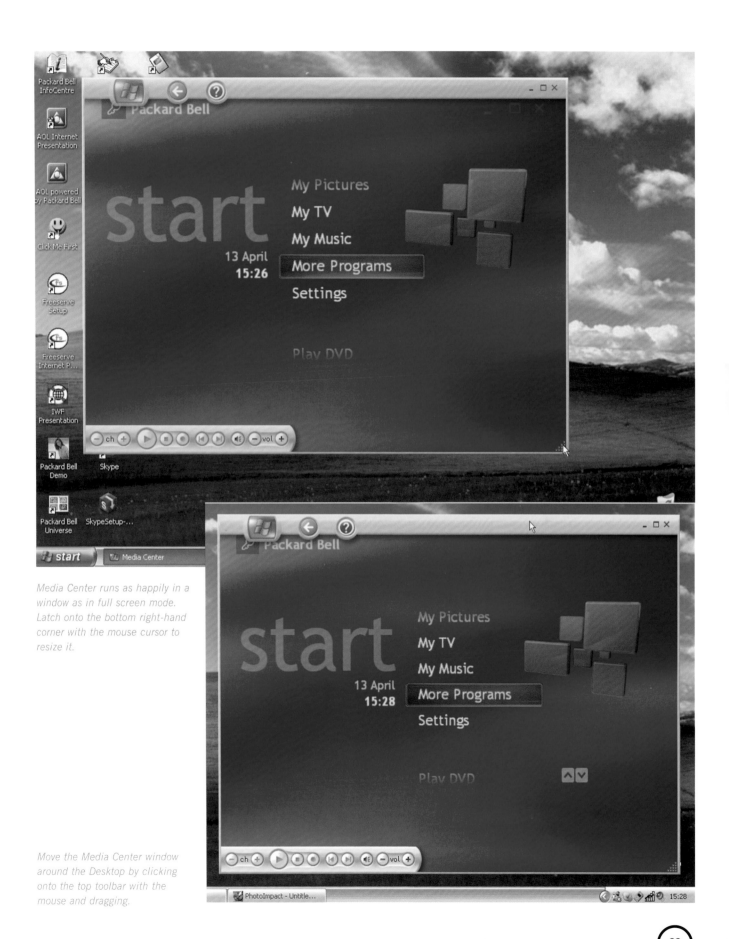

Media Center runs as happily in a window as in full screen mode. Latch onto the bottom right-hand corner with the mouse cursor to resize it.

Move the Media Center window around the Desktop by clicking onto the top toolbar with the mouse and dragging.

Display calibration

This procedure will help ensure that Media Center looks as good as it possibly can on your TV screen and makes the most of the available space.

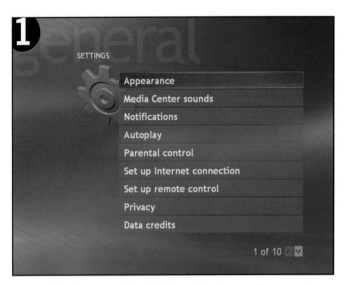

Scroll through the modules in the main menu until you reach Settings. Press OK on the remote to activate it. Now select General and press OK again. Next, select Appearance and press OK once more.

Some options. We suggest leaving Transition animations checked because we like the way menus fade and slide gently in and out, but you may prefer a snappier approach. The Window always on top option ensures that when Media Center is running in windowed mode, no other program is allowed to obscure it. This is contrary to the usual active-window-on-top approach in Windows and one, we suggest, to leave unchecked.

Use the down arrow to move through the options until TV is highlighted. Press OK to check the button. Use the left arrow now to highlight the Save button and press OK. The Media Center colours and brightness will change slightly now and you'll find yourself back at the Appearance menu option (Step 1). Check the TV screen. If you don't like this more muted effect, return to this screen and revert to the Computer monitor option. Now scroll down to select Adjust display settings and press OK.

An instructional video. Watching it is strictly optional but why not give it a whirl? Use the arrow keys to select the Watch video button and press OK. When you're through, you'll be returned to the Display Calibration screen. Highlight Next and continue.

An obvious choice. Think about your TV here, as this will be your primary display, and check the appropriate option. Of course, if your Media Center is not connected to a TV, in this and the following steps you should select the appropriate options for your monitor.

Equally obvious. Again, we are adjusting the settings for the TV, not the monitor, so select Widescreen if you have a widescreen TV and Standard if you don't.

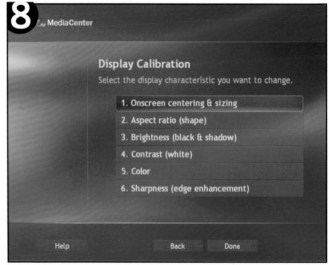

If your Media Center is connected to your TV via an S-Video or composite video cable, with or without a SCART adapter, select the first option here. The alternative would only apply if you're not using a TV at all or if the TV has a monitor-style interface (as LCD TVs typically do).

Six display options here and you should work your way through them all (you only have to do this once). In each case, you'll be prompted to watch a short video clip and invited to tweak your display settings. However, nothing in Media Center itself gets changed here: these steps simply allow you to configure your TV's settings (via its own remote) in order that the Media Center interface looks sharp, clear, centred and undistorted. If you're not familiar with how to modify your TV's display settings, now is the time to experiment.

When you're happy, or at least finished, click Done. This returns you to the screen you saw in Step 2. The Save button should be highlighted so press OK to confirm the changes and you'll find yourself back at Step 1. Job done. Return here at any time to alter your display settings.

Some other settings...

Aside from the Appearance business dealt with above, you might like to dip into one or two of the other options listed on the Settings menu. It's all pretty much self-explanatory but here's a quick guide:

- **Media Center sounds** Just sound effects when you select menu items, activate options and so forth, nothing more. We tolerate them; you may hate them.
- **Notifications** Popup messages from Windows.
- **Autoplay** Leave the defaults as they are to ensure that Media Center plays CDs and DVDs as soon as you pop a disc in the drive.
- **Parental control** Media Center allows you to control which types of DVD movie may be played. The system hinges on movie rating certificates – U, PG, 18 etc. – but for it to work a DVD has to a) be rated, and b) tell the computer what that rating is. In our experience, it usually doesn't work. However, there is a workaround that blocks all DVD movies at the outset. This is handy if you don't want your kids to be able to play any movies without your express permission.

First, enter a 4-digit code that your children won't automatically guess. Select DVD ratings from the mini-menu and press OK. In the next screen, highlight the Block unrated movies box and press OK to check it. This ensures that any DVD that either doesn't carry a rating or fails to tell Media Center what rating it is will be blocked by default. Also highlight the minus box and press OK a few times until the Maximum allowed movie rating is None. Highlight Save and press OK. Whenever you try to play a DVD movie in future, up will pop a prompt to enter your 4-digit parental code.

The Media Center Settings screen is home to global configuration options and repays a little exploration and tweaking.

However, we should point out that it remains perfectly possible to play the movie in the non-Media Center Windows environment with Windows Media Player or any other DVD playback software. In other words, and as always in computing, there are ways to circumvent parental controls if you are determined enough.

- **Set up Internet connection** This menu simply repeats the earlier wizard. It is no help in actually configuring an internet connection – for that, you need to work within Windows, as discussed on p.49 – but this is where to come if the Guide ever tells you that it's failed to download fresh data. Sometimes, reconfirming your settings and running the test option kick-starts the Guide back into action.
- **Set up remote control** A straight rerun of Step 4 on p.55. One to return to should your remote ever stop working (though we'd be inclined to change the batteries first).
- **Privacy** Opt in or out of the Guide here and read up on what Microsoft does with your data.
- **Data credits** Who does what behind the scenes
- **About Media Center** Version number and copyright details. Very dull.

Parental controls are useful for blocking DVDs but don't put too much faith in the software nanny.

Recording settings

Finally, a quick glance at a handful of other settings that you should be familiar with.

Return to the main Media Center menu – press the green button on your remote – and scroll through to Settings once again. Press OK and use the right arrow button to highlight TV and press OK again.

Highlight Recorder and press OK, then scroll down to Recording defaults and press OK again. You'll need to use the Channel/Page button to see all 9 options on this menu.

By way of explanation:

• **Keep** All Media Center PCs ship with huge hard disk drives but they eventually fill up. The default option here – Until space needed – means that Media Center keeps all recordings until disk space runs out, and then deletes the oldest first to make room for new recordings. The risk is that you could end up losing recordings before you've had the chance to watch them. To prevent this, select the Until I watch option. No unwatched recording will ever be deleted without your explicit say-so. Unfortunately, this also carries a different risk, namely that Media Center may not always find room for new recordings. Alternatively, you can select Until I delete. This stops Media Center from clearing out old recordings even after they have been watched. This is actually our preferred option because it puts control firmly in the hands of the user. It would be infuriating to discover that Media Center had scrubbed a favourite film before you'd had time to copy it to DVD, but it does mean you need to keep a watchful eye on disk space.

• **Quality** Fair, good, better or best. These settings determine the compression level applied to recordings, with a direct trade-off between quality and file size. Start off with the Best setting but if you find that you're scheduling more recordings than the hard disk drive can handle, and/or you're not getting around to archiving or deleting old shows, consider a shift down to Better or Good. Media Center will then be able to squeeze many more hours of video onto the drive. Note that you can always override this default setting for individual recordings (see p.89) so you may decide to use Better as the default, Best for films that you want to keep, and Good for watch-once sitcoms. Or whatever.

Settings accessed via this menu determine how Media Center handles TV recording.

• **Start when possible / Stop when possible** Useful 'padding' settings that tell Media Center to start and stop recording a few minutes before and after the scheduled programme slot. It's relatively rare for TV shows to begin earlier than billed but common for them to overrun. Unfortunately, you can only opt to record up to four minutes beyond the scheduled stop time. Still, it's better than nothing.

• **Language** If you want Media Center to record only English-language programmes, leave the default setting at English here. if you're happy for it to grab foreign language shows, change it to Any language.

• **Show type** This is the first of four options in the Series only recording defaults. As we have hinted, and as we shall soon see in practice, Media Center can record an entire series for you automatically e.g. grab every episode of *The Simpsons*. However, as you know only too well, broadcasters habitually show repeats. Indeed, it's common for two or more series to be shown in parallel. Partner channels Channel 4 and E4, for instance, may be broadcasting an old and new series of *Frasier* respectively in any given week. This option lets you specify whether Media Center should restrict itself to recording new episodes only (first runs) or whether it should also grab repeats (reruns). A third alternative, Live, restricts it further to recording only programmes broadcast live. This might be useful for sport or music programmes but it's too limiting to set as a default.

The choice is obviously yours but do bear in mind that Media Center is not psychic. That is, it can only make the right decisions based on information provided by the Guide, and that information is not faultless. Disk space permitting, our inclination is to grab first run and reruns by default. It's easy to delete superfluous episodes but frustrating to miss one episode in a new series because the Guide had it wrongly billed as a repeat. Besides, even oft-seen repeats can fill a dull evening when there's nothing else worth watching.

• **Record on** Rather confusing, this one. There are three possibilities: one channel only; one channel, anytime; and any channel, anytime. Remember that we are dealing with series recordings here and imagine that you want to record a series

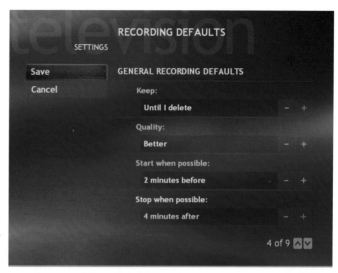

Here we have asked Media Center to record four minutes beyond the scheduled end of all programmes.

It's better to have too many episodes of a favoured series than too few.

called *The Simpsons*. As we'll see shortly, you would initiate this by selecting an episode from the Guide listings and scheduling a series recording. Let's say you select the first episode of a new series scheduled for broadcast at 7pm on Channel 29. Now, it is entirely possible that Channel 29 will broadcast the same episode twice or even thrice. If you select the One channel, anytime option, Media Center will record each showing. This means that you could end up with two or three copies of each episode.

If, however, you opt for One channel only, Media Center will only record episodes broadcast on Channel 29 at the time of the show you just selected. That is, it will record all episodes of *The Simpsons* shown on Channel 29 at 7pm and ignore repeats shown at 10am the following day. This is a safe selection if you are confident that the channel won't suddenly switch its broadcast schedule.

Deciding default settings for series recordings is a tricky business but you can always override them later. You can also visit the Scheduled Recordings screen to check that Media Center is primed to record all the right episodes (see p.95).

By contrast, the Any channel, anytime option tells Media Center to grab every episode of *The Simpsons* regardless of channel or broadcast time. If several channels are broadcasting *The Simpsons*, and if you instructed Media Center to record first runs and reruns, you could potentially end up with dozens of episodes.

Our recommendation is One channel, anytime, again on the basis that it's better to have a few unwanted episodes (although not too many) than risk missing one through an unscheduled change in transmission time.

- **Daily recording limit** Pre-empting the concerns just addressed, Media Center invites you to limit the recording of any series to one episode per day. In our imaginary example, Channel 29 broadcasts a repeat of the previous evening's show at 10am and then broadcasts a brand new episode at 7pm. With the Once per day selected, Media Center will record either the 10am or 7pm show, but not both. But which will it choose? Well, if you selected First run only above, it should ignore the 10am show, as this is technically a repeat. That, though, relies on the Guide data making this clear. Yet again, we prefer not to limit Media Center's freedom to record and recommend the No limit option.
- **Keep up to** Here you can instruct Media Center to delete older recordings when it reaches a given limit. The maximum is 10. Otherwise, select As many as possible and allow the settings discussed above to manage disk space.

Disk space

When you have made your changes, highlight Save and press OK. This returns you to the Recorder screen. Now select Recorder storage and press OK. This screen shows you at a glance how much recording time remains on your hard disk drive based on your chosen recording quality (you get another chance to alter this setting here). Because we are just setting out and the disk is virtually empty, we have over 42 hours to play with at the Better setting. This would reduce to 36 hours at Best, increase to 52 hours at Good and a massive 96 hours at the Fair setting. Return here at any time to check the Unused recording time figure, particularly when you suspect that disk space may be running short (i.e. when you have dozens of recordings stockpiled in your playlist pending deletion, burning to DVD or just viewing on a rainy afternoon).

The benefits of a gargantuan hard disk drive.

4

PART **4** PC HOME ENTERTAINMENT MANAUL

Media Center in action

PART 4 My TV

My TV is the module that most clearly sets Media Center apart from a standard Windows XP computer. It dramatically expands upon the usual capabilities of TV tuner software and turns the computer into a fully-fledged digital video recorder. It's easy to use, remarkably adept, and a fine and superior replacement for a VCR.

In this and the following chapters, we'll take a step-by-step approach to cover all the common things that you'll want to do.

Watch live TV

The most obvious use of My TV. We'll assume here and in the following pages that you've connected your Media Center to your TV set and, if relevant, set-top box according to the directions given earlier. Your TV should also be tuned to the appropriate audio-video channel i.e. the channel that displays the computer's output.

Press the green Start button on your Media Center remote control to bring up the main menu. If Media Center is currently running in windowed mode, revert to full screen. Use the right arrow button to highlight the middle of the three buttons in the top-right corner and press OK. You should find that My TV is already highlighted in the main menu, but if not just scroll through the options until it is. Click OK.

By default, Media Center displays the currently selected channel in a preview window. Try changing channels now using the remote. You can either tap in a channel number with the number pad or use the Channel/Page button. Settle on a channel that's currently broadcasting and you should see live pictures.

You should also be able to hear the selected channel through whichever speaker arrangement you opted for during setup, be it the TV's integrated speakers, separate stereo speakers or a full-blown surround sound system. Experiment with the volume button on the remote. Note the on-screen representation of the volume level. Aim to adjust your external speakers so that TV volume is acceptable at around the 12-15 mark on the Media Center control. From now on, you should be able to adjust the volume with the remote alone.

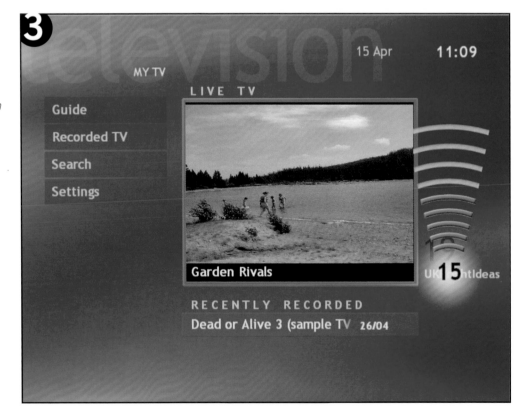

To watch TV in full screen mode without any Media Center menu encumbrance, use the arrow keys to highlight the preview window. When it is bordered in green, press OK and you'll see television pictures in full-screen mode. To return to the My TV menu and preview window, use the yellow My TV button on your remote. (You could go through the main menu but the Media Center remote has four useful shortcuts that take you straight to the central modules.) When you return to the menu, the Guide button on the left will be highlighted in readiness for you to access the Electronic Programme Guide. For now, though, press the right arrow once to highlight the preview window and activate full-screen TV once more.

While in full-screen television mode, press the More Info button on your remote. Along the bottom of the screen, you will see some helpful programme information. This is provided by and plucked from the Programme Guide. It's a handy way of quickly finding out what's currently being broadcast on any given channel without having to resort to a printed TV listings guide. Note that a More Info button within the information bar is pre-highlighted. Press OK on your remote to active it.

Here in the Programme Info screen, you can read further details about the current programme. You can also elect to record the programme or series, but we'll save that for a little later. For now, either activate the highlighted Play button to return to the live programme in full-screen mode, or use the Back button on your remote. We recommend spending some time alternating between the My TV menu, full-screen television, the More Info information bar and the Programme Info screen until it becomes second nature. Remember that you can always return to the main My TV menu by pressing the My TV button on your remote or to the main Media Center menu via the green Start button.

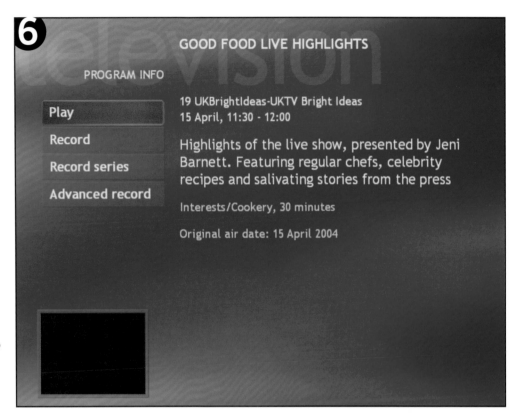

There may be occasions when you want to watch live television in a window while using your computer in standard Windows XP mode. This is easily and elegantly achieved. First, you must shift Media Center itself into windowed mode. If you have a mouse connected to your computer, as is likely if you are going to be using it in non-Media Center mode, you can call up the grey toolbar at any time simply by moving it slightly in any Media Center screen. Click the restore down button to reduce Media Center to a window, and drag it into the desired shape and position. Or, if you still have a keyboard plugged in, hit the Escape key to force Media Center into a window.

Alternatively, you can invoke windowed mode with the Media Center remote, but not, however, from within the My TV menu or when watching television full screen. Instead, you must return to the main menu – press the green Start button – and use the arrow keys to select the restore down button. (Note that the live TV channel continues to play in a preview window while you move around Media Center menus.) As we mentioned previously, you can't alter the size or position of the Media Center window without the help of a mouse.

With Media Center running in a window on your Windows Desktop, activate full-screen television as described above. The live programme will now fill the window. Press My TV and it returns to a preview window within the My TV menu, which itself fills the window. You can continue to use the remote to control Media Center while working with other Windows programs with the mouse and keyboard. When you want to restore Media Center to full screen, just click the maximise button.

The beauty of a buffer

When watching TV, there are several interesting options open to you. To appreciate why the following steps are possible, you have to understand that when you are watching 'live' TV through Media Center, you are actually watching a recording rather than the live broadcast itself. Behind the scenes, Media Center continually saves the live video stream (i.e. the current TV channel) to the hard disk drive as a digital file. What you see on screen is that file being played back almost instantaneously from the hard disk drive.

To see the buffer, press the Play button on your remote. Up pops an information bar with a timeline. The vertical black marker shows you your current position within the displayed time period, with the buffered recording appearing as the green shaded area to the left of the marker.

So what can you usefully do with a buffer?

Well, for one thing, you can use the buffer to replay live TV. As described on p.53, use the Rewind button to scroll back through the programme at different speeds, and the Replay button to skip backwards in 7-second skips. This is fantastically helpful for generating instant replays of anything that happens on screen: miss a goal and you can replay it to your heart's content. The thing to grasp here is that you can rewind or replay the current channel at any time i.e. you don't have to tell Media Center to buffer a channel; it does so automatically.

You can also pause a 'live' broadcast. Again, remember that what you are watching is a near-instant recording of the broadcast, not the live channel itself. Press the Pause button on your remote while watching any programme and it instantly freezes at the current frame, just as if you were pausing a video (which, in fact, is precisely what you are doing). Here, the marker shows that we paused the channel at 13.49. There were already several minutes of recorded video in the buffer (the shaded area to the left of the marker in the timeline) and the buffer is continuing to record the live channel beyond the pause point (the shaded area to the right of the marker).

In this screenshot, the current time is 13.24 and Media Center has buffered the previous five or six minutes of TV. This buffer will continue to build up to a maximum of 30 minutes.

13:49:43 ‖

13:00   14:00

13:56

Some important points:

- The buffer works on a rolling 30-minute cycle. This means that you can rewind or replay up to 30 minutes of the current channel. When the buffer fills up – i.e. when it has recorded a full 30 minutes – it continues to record the live channel; but for every new live minute recorded, a minute must be discarded from the beginning of the buffer.

- Media Center buffers the current channel whether or not you are actually watching it. That is, even when you are using Media Center to play a DVD or listen to music, the rolling buffer will still be recording whatever channel My TV happens to be tuned into. In fact, if you miss the beginning of a favourite show and My TV happens to be tuned to the appropriate channel, you can rewind and catch it from the beginning.

- While you are watching a rewound buffer period, Media Center continues to record the live broadcast. This means that you can either fast forward or skip ahead to catch up with the real-time broadcast – ad breaks are handy for this – or continue watching the buffered programme and, in effect, watch delayed live TV. However...

- If you change channels, the current buffer is lost and there's no way to get it back. This is a critical point to remember. For example, if you happen to be watching Channel 29 ten minutes behind real time – i.e. replaying a ten-minute buffer – and you hop to Channel 30 for just a moment, when you return to Channel 29 the buffer will be gone and you'll find yourself watching real-time live TV. Media Center will start a fresh buffer but those lost ten minutes are gone forever. It is thus good practice to catch up with the live broadcast as soon as possible.

- Also, and alas, you cannot buffer one channel while watching another.

We appreciate that on paper this buffer stuff all sounds rather complicated, but you'll soon get the hang of it for real. In particular, the first time you realise that you can pause a programme while you answer the door or telephone or make a cup of tea – and pick up exactly where you left off without missing a moment – will be a revelation.

From a pause point, you can press Play to resume watching the channel from where you left off, or skip backwards or forwards through the buffer.

PART **Getting started with recording**

There's no great mystery to hard-disk-drive-based video recording. Basically, the Media Center PC saves a live TV broadcast as a video file. Once saved, the file can be played back at any time. You can record a live channel while you're watching it, schedule the recording of any TV programme up to two weeks in advance, or record an entire series automatically.

DVR-MS

We saw on p.67 that you can customise the recording quality in Media Center and mentioned that the outcome of this choice is reflected in file size. Here's the equation in more detail (using Microsoft figures):

Recording Quality	Approximate file size per hour
Best	3GB
Better	2.5GB
Good	2GB
Fair	1GB

Programmes are actually recorded in a proprietary file format called DVR-MS. This is essentially the MPEG-2 video format with added potential to incorporate digital rights management (DRM) technology that can prevent television programmes from being indiscriminately copied and illegally distributed. It certainly complicates the issue of archiving recordings to DVD, as we shall see, and even has a bearing on whether you can watch recordings on other computers. However, if all you want to do is record TV programmes, watch them on the Media Center and eventually delete them, it's plain sailing.

Record live TV

While watching any channel, press the Record button on your Media Center remote. That's it: the current programme will be automatically saved to the hard disk drive. In fact, it was already being saved in the buffered form discussed a moment ago, but activating the record function saves it as a 'proper' file rather than a cycling buffer. Five points to note:

- Recording starts the moment you press the button and does not include any buffered material. If you missed the first ten minutes of a film but you know that the buffer stretches back to the beginning of the show, you have a bit of a dilemma. If you press record, Media Center will save the rest of the film from this point on but those first ten minutes will not be included in the recording.

- Importantly, and very unfortunately in our view, this is true even if you rewind to the beginning of the buffer before pressing Record. You might expect that Media Center would then include the buffered ten minutes in the final file, but sadly no: the recording still begins in real time and the start of the film is lost. What's more, the buffer itself is sacrificed and you'll find yourself watching the film in real time with no way to rewind back to the beginning. Just something to be aware of!

- The recording will automatically end when the current programme ends (or rather when it is scheduled to end according to the Guide listings data). This means you can hit the Record button and leave the computer unattended without worrying that it will continue recording the channel (and filling up your hard disk drive) until you tell it to stop. Or, of course, you can press the Stop button at any time, in which case Media Center will ask you to confirm your decision.

Media Center saves TV recordings in a single folder. Its default location, or address, is: C:\Documents and Settings\All Users\Documents\Recorded TV.

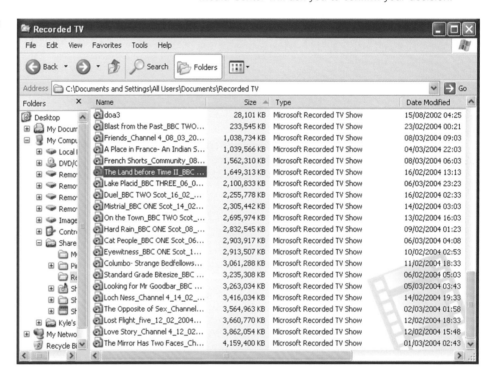

Press Record and the current programme on the current channel will be saved as a digital video file to the hard disk drive.

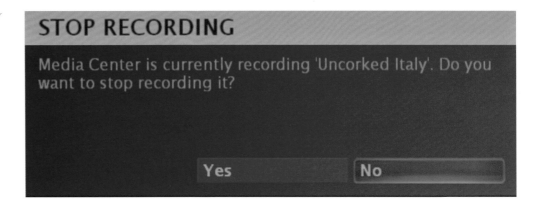

STOP RECORDING

Media Center is currently recording 'Uncorked Italy'. Do you
want to stop recording it?

| Yes | No |

● You cannot record one channel while watching another.
Likewise, you cannot change channels away from the channel
that Media Center is recording once it has started (if you try,
you have to cancel the current recording first). This is actually
a serious limitation with Media Center and one you should be
well aware of. The problem is that the computer has a single
TV tuner, which effectively means that it can only receive and
record one television channel at any given time.

Compare and contrast this with using a standard VCR, if you
will. Here, you can happily watch BBC1, say, while recording
BBC2. The reason is that the VCR has its own integrated TV
tuner and so can record any live channel quite independently
of what appears on the television screen. It comes as quite
some surprise to find that you can't do the same in the
supposedly more advanced digital age.

True, as we suggested back on p.40, you can split an
incoming TV signal and connect it to both your Media Center
(perhaps via a set-top box) and to your television. This gives
you some added flexibility: while the Media Center is busy
recording one channel through its TV tuner, you can at least

watch one of the five terrestrial analogue channels on the
television set independently of the computer. In fact, you could
even add a VCR to the mix.

It's far from ideal, though, and we hope that future versions of
Media Center will support dual TV tuners. This is already the
norm with the second series of TiVo devices (hard disk drive
recorders with PVR functionality) in the US and with Sky Plus
recorders in the UK. You cannot simply add a second TV tuner
to your computer, incidentally, as Media Center simply doesn't
support (work with) such a hardware configuration.

● On the upside, you can record a live television channel while
watching a pre-recorded show in Media Center, or indeed
while playing a DVD, listening to music or enjoying a picture
slideshow. Also bear in mind that many programmes are
repeated on TV, particularly on the digital channels. When
there is a clash between two programmes that you want to
watch, search the Guide to see if one or other is scheduled for
a repeat in the near future. If so, the best bet is to schedule a
recording for that show and watch the other programme now.

From the My TV screen, select a recent recording or use the Recorded TV link to see the lot.

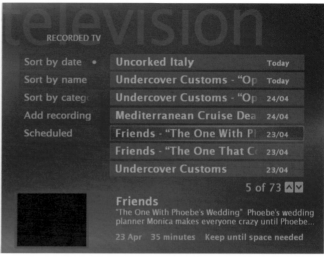

Scroll, sort and select recordings here.

Options aplenty: play, delete or manage a recording.

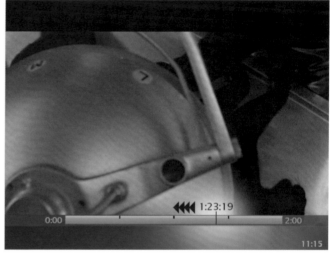

When pausing or altering playback settings, a buffer-style timeline shows you where you are in relation to the start and finish. Here, we are rewinding from just before the three-quarters mark.

Play a recording

As soon as you have recorded a programme, you can play it back in Media Center. Press the My TV button on your remote. Below the preview window, you'll see a short list of the most recent recordings. Use the arrow keys to select one and press OK to start playback. Alternatively, for a full list of all recorded shows, select the Recorded TV button on the left.

You can sort recordings by date, name or category (see p.94), and scroll through the list with the up/down arrows or Channel/Page button on your remote. Helpfully, recordings are automatically saved with programme names and appended with the date of the recording.

Select any recording and press OK (or More Info) to see a Program Info screen with full programme details culled from the Programme Guide. To the left are some obvious options. Select Play to play the recording immediately; Delete to delete it unwatched;

or Keep until... to access the options first seen on pp.66–67. This last one is useful if earlier you selected Keep until space needed as the default storage option for recordings, as now you have a chance to override the default to ensure that a particularly precious programme is not discarded for the sake of disk space.

The Record series or Series info buttons – you see the former when you have selected a show that isn't already part of a scheduled series recording and the latter for one that is – let you schedule or modify series recordings from here (but see also p.90).

Alternatively, highlight any recording in the Recorded TV menu and press the Play button on your remote to begin playback immediately without seeing these options.

During playback, you can pause, rewind, fast forward, replay and skip through the programme.

You can also use the Stop button, naturally enough, to stop

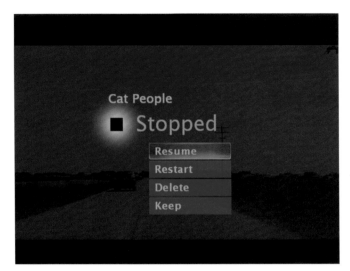

When you press Stop, the Resume option continues playback from the current point; and Restart takes you back to the beginning. This is often quicker than rewinding through the entire length of a video.

Yet another chance to ensure that Media Center doesn't overwrite a half-watched programme with a new recording.

Thanks to the preview window, you can continue to watch a recording (or live TV) while browsing menus and making selections.

There's no need to figure out where you left off watching a recording last time around — Media Center remembers this for you.

playback, at which point you'll be given the choice of resuming, restarting, deleting or keeping the recorded programme.

If you want to watch the rest of the recording later, select Keep. You'll now see the Keep Until screen with a full range of options. A new entry here – Don't change – will be highlighted. Press OK to save the recording unchanged and return to the Program Info screen. From here, click the Back button to return to the main My TV menu. Alternatively, modify the Keep until... settings for this particular programme.

If you just want to save a recording for later resumption and don't need to change any settings, just press the My TV button immediately after stopping playback.

In fact, you can also press My TV during playback to call up the My TV menu (and from there perhaps move to Recorded TV to select a different programme). Until you select an alternative

recording, the recording you were watching continues to play in a preview window.

Finally, when you stop a recording and return to it later from the Recorded TV menu, Media Center invites you to resume playback from where you left off. This is very handy, particularly with films and other long programmes. If you want to watch the whole programme from the beginning, simply rewind or press Stop followed by Restart.

Note again that you can watch recorded programmes while Media Center is busy recording live television. Live recording simply continues in the background, out of sight. This is possible because the computer can write to and read from the hard disk drive simultaneously i.e. save a new file (the live channel) and play an existing file (any recording) at the same time. Clever things, hard disk drives.

PART  # The Programme Guide and scheduled recordings

If all you could do was record live TV channels, the Media Center would make a pretty poor replacement for a VCR. But of course you can do much, much more than that. This is the territory of the Electronic Programme Guide – downloadable detailed TV listings that provide a fortnight's programme information in advance and enable all manner of useful PVR (Personal Video Recorder) features.

EPG for free

On a point of interest, when TiVo launched in the UK back in late 2000, it offered a very similar style of EPG-based recording. In fact, Media Center's My TV module is in many ways a clone of TiVo. However, TiVo operated on a subscription basis and it cost £10 per month to use the EPG. Data was downloaded in a daily (free) phone call, so the hardware had to be connected to a telephone line. This additional cost was, we suspect, one of the reasons for TiVo's ultimate failure in the UK (well, that and a lousy marketing campaign).

You can still buy TiVos second-hand, particularly on eBay, and the EPG subscription is still up and running, although handled these days by Sky.

as recommended by sky digital

To Do List

⊙	Sat	16/12	7.00 pm	Sky One	Smash Hits Poll...
☑	Sat	16/12	8.30 pm	BBC1	Airport
☑	Sun	17/12	8.00 pm	Sky One	The Simpsons
☑	Sun	17/12	8.30 pm	PARCOM	Frasier
☑	Mon	17/12	10.00 pm	BBC2	Human Remains
☑	Mon	18/12	10:30 pm	UKSTY	House in France
☑	Tue	18/12	8.00pm	BBC1	Animal Hospital
☑	Wed	19/12	9.00pm	Sky One	Star Trek: Voyager

Be thankful for a free EPG. Of course, you're paying for it in the cost of your Media Center PC but at least there's no ongoing subscription.

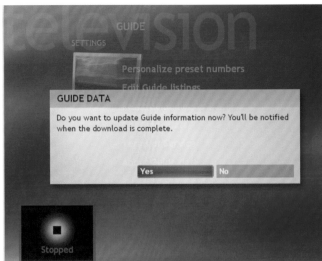

Update your data at any time. This isn't usually necessary if you have a broadband internet connection.

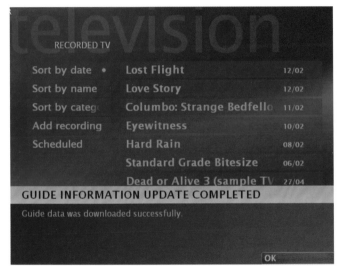

Success.

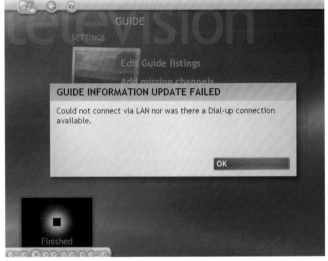

Failure.

With Media Center, you get your programme guide for free. Whether it will continue thus forever, we cannot say. You do need an internet connection to download the data but that's about it: listings are automatically and seamlessly incorporated within the Media Center interface. Compare and contrast with the ShowShifter EPG options discussed later!

Forcing a Guide update

We looked at the Programme Guide schedule settings earlier (pp.60–61) but you can force a fresh download at any time. This is useful if your Media Center has been offline for a while and only has a few days' worth of data remaining. Sometimes Media Center will prompt you to initiate a download but otherwise take the reins yourself. Return to the main Media Center menu – press the green Start button on your remote – and select Settings, TV and Guide. Now highlight the Get Guide data option and press OK. Press OK again when prompted to confirm that you want to update the listings. The download will now proceed in the background. This can take quite a while over a modem, but you can freely work elsewhere within Media Center while it's in progress.

If you stay at the Guide screen, however, you'll eventually see confirmation that the download has been successful.

Or not. Sometimes it fails and you have to try again later. Sometimes (in our experience, anyway), Media Center tells you that there is no available internet connection, even when you've already run through the Setup wizard and know perfectly well that there is.

It's a frustrating business. We've found that restarting Media Center usually does the trick. Alternatively, try the mini-wizard at Settings, General and Set up Internet connection. If that doesn't work, reboot the computer. Or – and this works best of all – be patient and try downloading the updates again later.

Using the Program Guide

Press the green Start button on your remote, then select My TV and Guide. This takes you straight into the TV listings. Alternatively, use the dedicated Guide button on your remote.

The Guide always opens at the current time. To the left is a vertical list of channels and to the right their respective programme listings. These are shown on a horizontal timeline with the timescale along the top. Getting around is easy, as we shall now discover.

Time and date of programme listings currently being viewed.

Current time.

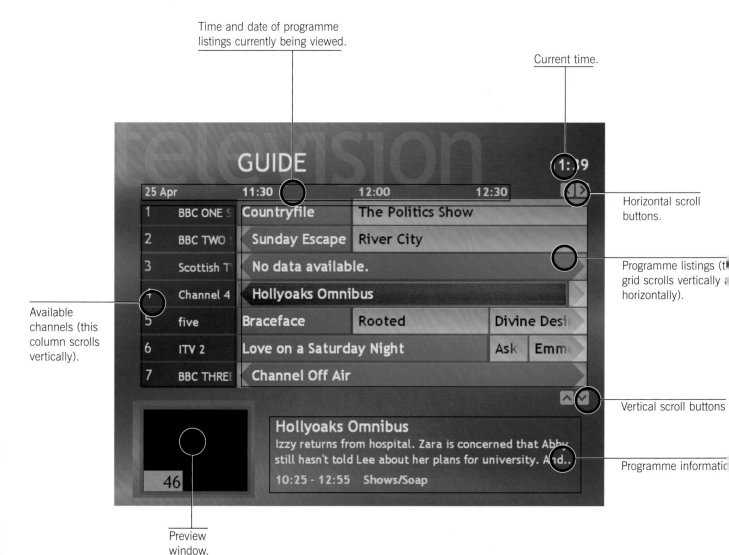

Horizontal scroll buttons.

Programme listings (the grid scrolls vertically and horizontally).

Available channels (this column scrolls vertically).

Vertical scroll buttons

Programme information

Preview window.

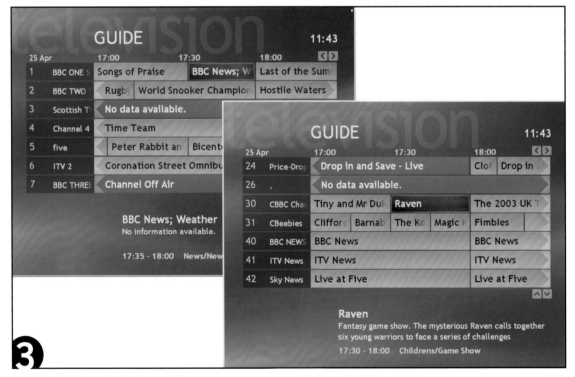

1 Unless you are restricted to the five analogue channels, you won't be able to see all available channels on the same screen. To see others, highlight any channel in the left-hand column and use the up and down arrow buttons to scroll through the channel list. You can also use the Channel/Page button to jump up and down a 'page' at a time.

2 You can see at a glance which programmes are being broadcast right now on any visible channels, plus what's on over the next hour or so (just how far ahead you see depends on whether or not you have a widescreen TV: see p.67). To see future listings, use the right arrow button to move from the channel column into the programme listings and then press it repeatedly to skip through the listings a half hour at a time.

3 You can also use the up and down arrow buttons to scroll through channels in the listings section. Here, for example, we have scrolled horizontally through the BBC1 listings to 17.30 (the News is on then), and then scrolled down to see what's on channel numbers 24 through to 42 at the same time (Raven is on Channel 30). We can now continue to scroll horizontally and vertically to view more programme listings at different times or on different channels. To scroll more quickly through the listings,

use the Fast Forward button. This jumps ahead three hours at a time e.g. you can get from 07.00 to 21.00 with four button presses. The Rewind button works the same way in reverse. You can also use the Skip button to fly through the listings twelve hours at a time e.g. from 07.00 to 21.00 with one move. The Replay button scrolls backwards in 12-hour chunks. Remember that you can look up to 14 days in advance, depending on the freshness of your Programme Guide data.

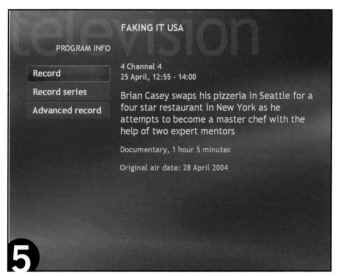

4 To see what's on one particular channel, highlight that channel in the channels' column and press OK. This calls up a dedicated screen that shows you the current and future listings for that channel only. In this example, we have selected Channel 4. The current programme is Hollyoaks Omnibus, followed at 12.55 by Faking it USA. Media Center tells us that it has information about 355 forthcoming programmes and we can scroll through the lot using the up and down arrow or Channel/Page buttons.

5 Whenever a programme is highlighted in the Guide, either in the dedicated channel screen just mentioned or in the main listings view, brief information about it appears just below the listings. To view more detailed information, press OK while the programme is highlighted. This takes you to a page containing full programme details and some recording options. We'll return to it in a moment. Meanwhile, to return to the Guide, use the Back button.

6 Let's imagine that you're currently watching BBC1 in full-screen mode and the current programme is about to finish. You wonder what's on next. Rather than reaching for a printed guide in a newspaper or magazine, simply press the Guide button on your remote and scroll vertically through the programme listings. BBC1 will continue to play in a preview window so you don't miss anything. Highlight any other current programme on a different channel, press OK, and Media Center will change channels and play that programme full-screen. Or, to return immediately to the show you were watching without changing channels, press the Back button or the Live TV button (the latter always takes you immediately to full-screen mode).

7 We've looked already at how to initiate a recording when watching live TV – see p.80 – but you can also start or schedule recordings directly from the guide. To record a live programme – that is any programme currently being broadcast on any available channel – highlight it in the guide and press Record. Without further ado, Media Center changes channel and starts recording that programme. The live programme plays in the preview window and the Guide entry is flagged with a red circle icon. Highlight the preview window and press OK to watch the programme full screen (or simply press OK while the programme remains highlighted in the Guide).

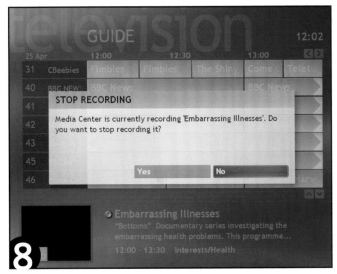

8

The recording will stop either when the programme finishes or when you press Stop. In the latter case, you will be asked to confirm that you really want to cancel the recording. The default reply is no, so press OK if you made a mistake and really want to continue. If you do wish to cancel the recording, use the left arrow to highlight Yes, and press OK. The partial recording will be saved in your Recorded TV menu (see p.82), from where you can watch or delete it.

9

To record a future programme, do just the same thing: find the programme in the Guide, select it, and press Record. Assuming that there is no conflict with another scheduled recording, Media Center will flag the programme for future recording. So long as the computer is turned on or in standby mode when that programme comes on, Media Center will record it automatically.

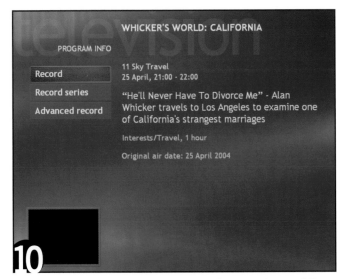

10

Alternatively, select a programme in the Guide and press OK. This takes you to the Programme Information page and offers three recording choices. The first, Record, has exactly the same effect as pressing the Record button when the programme is highlighted in the Guide, as just described. We'll come to the second, Record series, shortly.

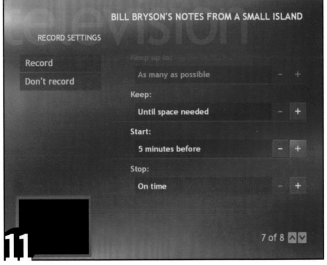

11

The third option is Advanced recording. Here you get the opportunity to override the default padding times, the Keep Until setting and, importantly, the recording quality level. As we said earlier, you may wish to use Better or Good as the default recording quality (decent picture; medium file size) but switch to Best (great picture; larger files) for films and favourite programmes. Changes made, select the Record button to schedule the recording.

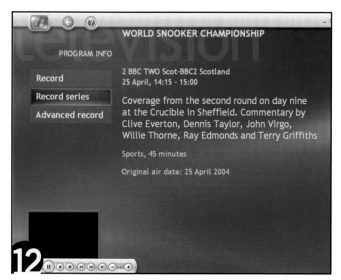

One of the great plus points of the Media Center is its ability to record an entire series automatically. Simply highlight any episode of any series in the Guide, press OK, and select Record series. All future episodes will now be recorded without further question according to the choices you made earlier (see pp.67–69).

When you have scheduled a programme recording, that programme is differentiated in the Guide listings with a red circle icon. When you have scheduled a series recording, each episode is flagged with three red circles. These icons help you see and remember Media Center's future duties when browsing the Guide.

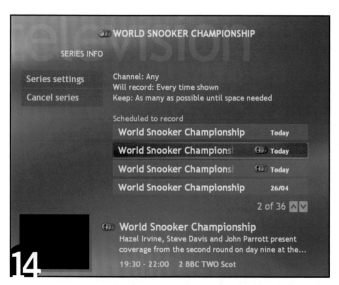

If you'd like to see further details about a scheduled series recording, highlight an episode in the Guide and press OK. A new option, Series info, appears. Select this to see a summary of Media Center's default recording settings and a chronological list of broadcast times and channel details for each forthcoming episode. You can remove any given episode from this list or otherwise modify its individual recording settings. You can also select Series settings to override the default settings configured earlier (pp.67–69) for this particular series. Select Cancel series to scrub the entire series recording. Note that conflicts are flagged with an exclamation mark in a red circle. When you see this, you know that this particular episode will not be recorded unless you take steps to resolve the conflict.

Say you schedule a recording for a one-hour programme on Channel 29 beginning at 21.00 on Thursday. A little later, you attempt to record a programme on Channel 30 scheduled to start at 21.30 on the same evening. Media Center cannot record both, so it asks you to resolve the conflict. There are a couple of possibilities here. If one or other programme is going to be repeated within the lifetime of Media Center's Guide data, it should offer you the option to reschedule that recording accordingly. Failing this, you have to choose which of the programmes to ditch. Use the up and down arrows to toggle between the options, noting which programme will and which one won't record. Welcome to life with a single TV tuner.

You can also highlight any conflict-flagged programme in the Guide, press OK and select the Record option. This provides a second chance to see what programme it conflicts with and decide how to resolve the clash.

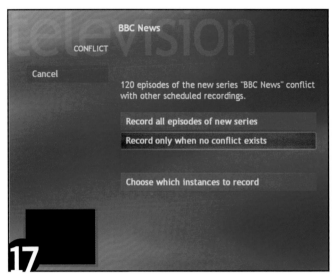

Conflict resolution is best done at the time of scheduling a series recording. At this point, you'll be warned about known conflicts and invited to choose how to proceed. If you want to record every episode of the new series at whatever cost, simply select the Record all episodes of new series. Take care, though, as you may now miss some other treasured show. The alternative option – Record only when no conflict exists – is fine if you don't mind missing the odd episode.

The best bet, though, is selecting Choose which instances to record and working your way through the list of conflicts. Media Center will show you each programme clash in chronological order and let you specify which programme to record and which to skip.

19

It's also possible to schedule recordings remotely as if you were using a VCR. Although it's not immediately obvious why you would want to bother with any of this given the point-and-click convenience of the Programme Guide, we can think of three good reasons. First, Guide date is not always 100% reliable and you may be aware of a late-breaking programme schedule change that is not reflected in the listings. In this case, you should manually configure a recording without reference to the incorrect Guide. Secondly, the Guide data doesn't always include regional variations. For instance, we found it impossible to get listings for Scottish TV (the Scottish version of ITV). Here, you may have no option but to work manually. Finally, manual recording is the best way to ensure that you capture the entire action when you suspect a programme may overrun. Sporting

events are obvious candidates. Instead of relying on the maximum four-minute padding, schedule a manual recording to conclude perhaps an hour after the scheduled programme end. (An alternative is to include the following programme(s) in a scheduled recording.) Remember, Media Center doesn't actually 'know' what's on or what it's recording: it merely follows orders and records a stated channel between stated times, labelling it according to the listings data in the Guide.

20. To schedule a recording manually, go to the main My TV menu – use the shortcut button on your remote – and select Record TV. Now select Add recording, and finally select the Channel and time option.

21

Use the remote control buttons to navigate around the various fields here and make selections. For instance, to change the date, use the arrow keys to highlight the + sign in the date field and press OK repeatedly until the correct date is shown. To configure the start and end times, move the highlighter into the fields and use the number pad to enter times. Don't forget to set the correct channel.

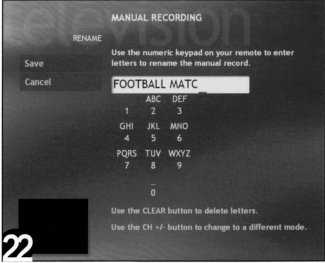

22

When your settings are complete, select the add title option and give your recording a name. This requires mobile-phone-style multi-tapping again (see p.52), but it's worth it as what you enter here determines how the show appears in the Recorded TV menu later. Finally, select Record.

The Programme Guide can be a vast and complex database, particularly if you have a cable or satellite TV service. Even with Freeview, trying to find a programme by browsing alone can be tiresome. Thankfully, though, the Guide can be searched and queried in a number of 'intelligent' ways. Press the My TV button on your Media Center remote and select the Search button from the on-screen menu. You now have three main search options, which we'll look at in turn.

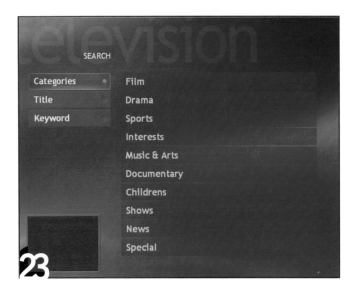

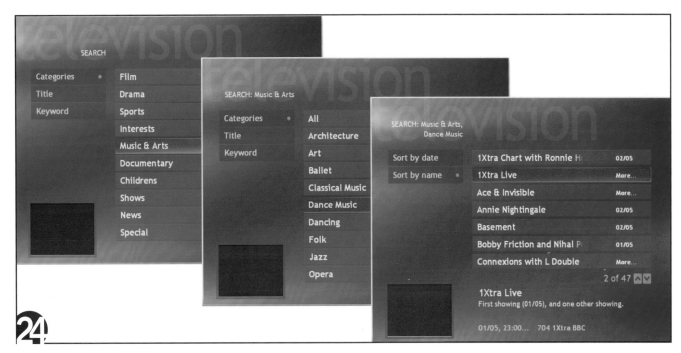

The Categories option lists programmes according to type. This is handy if you want to see which films or sports are on during the next fortnight, say, or to record children's shows. Each entry leads to a sub-menu with more specific choices. For instance, the Music & Arts category opens up to include entries for Architecture, Ballet, Folk, Jazz and several others. When you select one of the sub-menu entries, you'll be shown a complete list of all programmes that fit that criteria. Scroll through the listings with the arrow buttons (or Channel/Page button) to see

the full list. Or, if there are too many programmes to browse comfortably, use the menu options on the left to select shows by date (soonest first) or by name (alphabetically).

At any time, select a programme by highlighting it and pressing OK, and you'll be taken to the Programme Info menu. Here you can read more about the programme and schedule a recording. Work your way back through the menus and sub-menus using the Back button.

Obviously enough, the Title page lets you find programmes by name. The tricky part is that you have to use the alphanumeric keypad on the remote (see p.52). To find a show called The Food Programme, for instance, requires the following actions (or, of course, a keyboard):

Button	No. of presses	Resulting letter
8	1	
Enter	1	T
4	2	
Enter	1	H
3	2	
Enter	1	E
0	1	
Enter	1	Space
3	3	
Enter		F
6	3	
Enter		O
6	3	
Enter		O
3	1	
Enter		D

That only gets you as far as 'The Food' but that should be sufficient. To the right of the Title field, you'll see a list of all programmes beginning with those words (there may be only the one, as in this screenshot). Use the right arrow button to move the highlighter into the list, scroll up and down if necessary to find the correct programme, highlight it, and press OK. Now you can view all upcoming episodes.

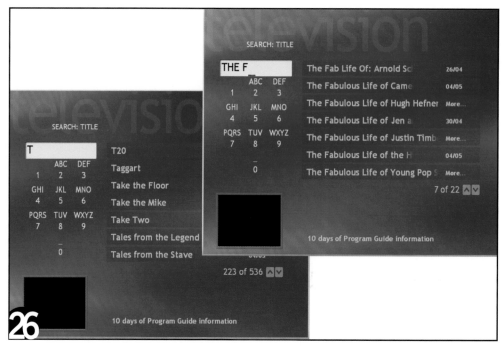

You don't actually have to use the Enter key between letters so long as you allow a sufficient pause for the cursor to move to the next position. In fact, if your next letter requires a different number button to the one you just used – e.g. when moving from the 8/T button to 4/H – you don't even need the pause. If you make a mistake, use the Clear button to backtrack one letter at a time (don't use the Back button). As soon as you start entering letters, Media Center starts filtering results. Here, when we enter the first T, the list on the right shows 536 'hits' i.e. 536 programmes or episodes with titles beginning with the letter 'T'. Adding an H reduces this to 400, and an E to 373. The space makes no difference, as you would expect, but beginning the second word with an 'F' narrows the hits down to 22. At this point, it would be easier to stop 'typing' and start scrolling through the hits.

The Keyword option uses a similar filtering technique but is broader in scope. You might, for instance, enter the word 'food' to find The Food Programme. *Importantly, though, this filter includes programme information culled from the Guide, so you'll be given a list of programmes about food as well as those that include 'food' in their titles. It can be rather idiosyncratic with some truly tenuous results – keyword 'food' returned an episode of* Dilbert *in which he 'tries to sell a new food to the country of Elbonia' – but it's also a tremendously useful way of finding programmes that interest you. Just enter any keyword you fancy and see what Media Center throws back at you. Chances are you'll uncover some gems that you never knew were on.*

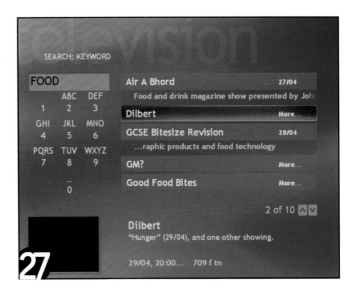

You can easily view – and modify – scheduled recording settings. Return to My TV and select the Recorded TV button. Now select the Scheduled button from the menu on the right to see a summary of all pending recordings. If you want to change or delete a recording, select it and work through the options. You can also sort listings by name or by category. Again, the icon next to the programme title tells you whether you're dealing with a one-off or a series recording.

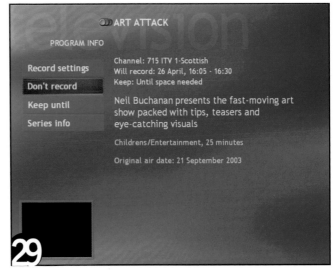

To change recording settings or to cancel a recording, simply highlight the programme in this list (or in the main Guide) and press OK. You'll now see a Don't record button that instantly cancels the scheduled recording, along with a Record settings button that takes you to all the usual options.

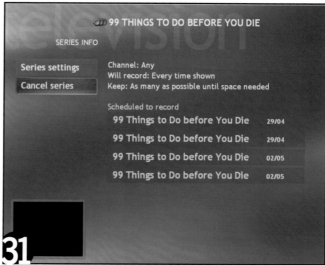

If the programme is part of a series, you can choose to modify settings for this particular episode alone or for the entire series.

If you want to call off a scheduled series recording in one easy move, select Series info from the Scheduled menu (shown in Step 29). On the following screen, just select Cancel series.

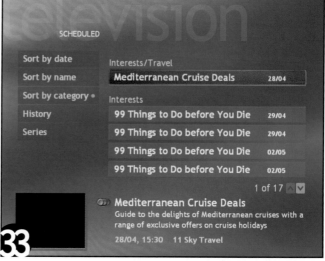

While in the Scheduled menu – see Step 28 – note the History button. This is a useful way of checking which programmes you have recorded in the past. It comes in handy if you know you recorded a programme that you enjoyed once but can no longer remember what it was called. Again, the list can be sorted for easy navigation.

The Series button – a further option in the Scheduled screen – provides yet another quick way to view, sort and edit scheduled series-only recordings. Select any series and quickly cancel recording or modify its recording settings.

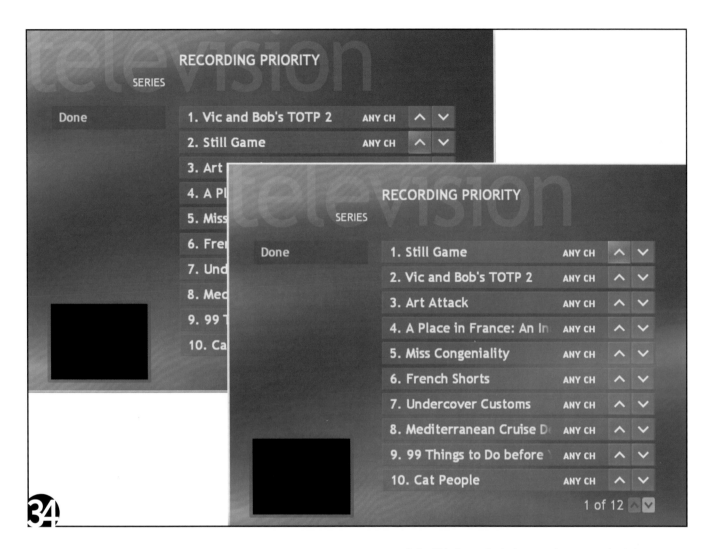

Finally, there's another way of determining that one series will definitely get recorded in the event of an unresolved conflict with another. As already discussed, you get an opportunity to resolve known conflicts when you first schedule a recording, but new conflicts can crop up at any time, perhaps even weeks down the line.

It's a simple enough technique: start in My TV and select Recorded TV > Scheduled > Series > Change priorities. This calls up a complete list of all scheduled series recordings. When Series A is higher up the priority list than Series B, Series A automatically gets recorded in the event of a conflict with Series B. It's thus well worthwhile coming to this screen to ensure that favoured programmes have the best chance of being recorded

successfully. This is particularly true when you schedule new series recordings, as these are always added to the bottom of the list by default.

To shuffle priorities, use the up and down arrows to scroll through the list. To move a series up a spot, for instance, highlight the upwards-pointing arrow button next to its title and press the OK button. The list will shuffle one space accordingly. To move it up another spot, press OK again. To demote a series, use the down-pointing button, and so forth. In this screenshot, we have moved Still game to the top of the tree. The idea is to create a priority list that reflects the importance you attach to each series. It's fiddly, yes, but one day we'll warrant you'll be grateful that the option is there.

PART ④ My Music

If you can master My TV, you should have no difficulty with the rest of Media Center. We'll be shortly be skimming through My Pictures and My Videos. First, though, we need to investigate the powerful My Music module.

It's a mixed affair. On one hand, My Music turns the Media Center computer into a powerful jukebox, a veritable hi-fi replacement, equally adept at playing CDs and MP3s and indeed making no real distinction between the two. Music can be sorted and searched, you can create playlists manually or automatically, it's possible to play music files located on a different computer (assuming you have a network), and you can copy CDs to the hard disk drive. Media Center will even download CD information and play some psychedelic effects on your TV screen.

On the other hand, however, My Music is really just a bolt-on interface for the Windows Media Player 9 application, which is itself supplied with Windows. The upshot is that you occasionally must revert to a Windows XP environment in order to get the most out of My Music – and that involves using the mouse and keyboard that we were so keen to be rid of earlier.

Ho hum. What can we say? We expect that My Music will evolve to more neatly mesh with the rest of Media Center but for now we have to talk you through the way it is, for better or worse.

Preparing Windows Media Player for action

You might prefer to perform these steps during initial setup while you still have a keyboard, mouse and monitor connected to your Media Center PC. Remember, this action occurs within Windows XP, so close Media Center before you begin.

A word about Media Library. This is the Windows Media Player application's rather unintuitive method of managing music. From the program's perspective and, later, from within Media Center, it doesn't much matter where music is physically located or even what form it is in so long as Media Library can find it. By default, Media Library knows to look for tracks in the My Music folder – a sub-folder of My Documents – and will automatically catalogue any files it finds there. It thus makes sense to move any existing music files to My Music right at the outset.

However, you can also tell Windows Media Player to search for files held in other locations, including different folders, drives and (assuming you have a network) computers.

Launch Windows Media Player from the Start menu, click the Tools button and select Options. In the Privacy tab, tell the program how you want to handle music. We suggest checking all three of the Enhanced Playback Experience boxes, as these make your music files more amenable to Media Center's search and filter tools. It also ensures that you can play protected content downloaded from the internet. We're not too keen on sending unique identification to content providers, though.

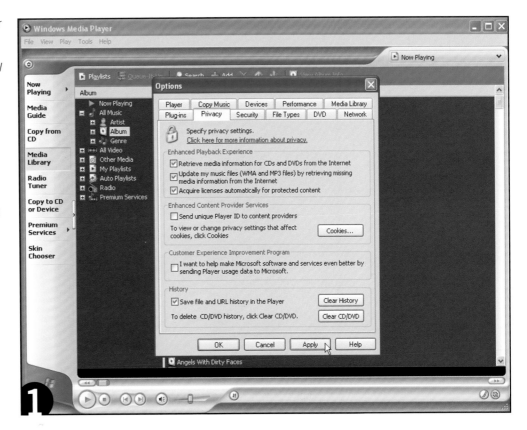

Now open the File Types tab and check all the boxes. This simply ensures that Windows Media Player can play more or less anything you throw at it. Also look in the Media Library tab and check the Overwrite existing information field. This grants Windows Media Player permission to update erroneous ID3 tags with correct data. If, however, you are confident that your music collection is already well catalogued, select the Only add missing information option to safeguard existing ID3 tags. If you don't know what ID3 tags are, incidentally, they'll soon prove very important. See p.102 and Appendix 2 for details.

Open the Copy Music tab and determine how Windows Media Player (and thus Media Center) will copy audio CDs. The default file format is Windows Media Audio, similar to the more popular MP3 format, at a bit rate of 128Kbps. We suggest moving the slider to the right to the 192Kbps mark. Each copied CD will now require more disk space – around 86MB compared to 56MB at 128Kbps – but will sound better.

Incidentally, you can force Windows Media Player to rip in the MP3 format but only if you pay for a third-party plug-in. Click the Learn more about MP3 formats link for details and pricing (this requires an internet connection).

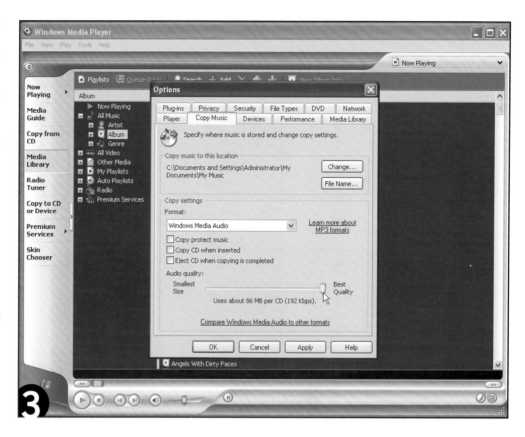

Now return to the main program and click the Media Library option on the left. You may be presented with a mini-wizard at this point that prompts you to search for available music files. Failing that, use the Add button (look for a little green plus-sign icon) and select By Searching Computer.

In the first field, tell Windows Media Player where to look for music on this computer. If you have files scattered across different folders, select the Local Drives, minus program folders option. If you have already moved everything to My Music, select the My Music Folder option instead.

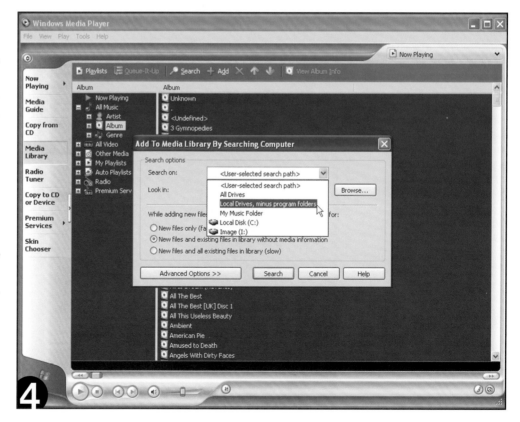

If your Media Center is connected to a network, and if a computer on the network has music files that you would like to play on the Media Center, there's no need to move them to the Media Center itself. Instead, you can stream them across the network. This works most reliably over a wired network but with a fair wind you should fare OK over a wireless network.

For this to work, you must first share the networked folder in order that the Media Center can access it. This is a standard networking procedure. Now tell Media Library where to find it. Use the Browse button next to the Look in: field and navigate to the shared network folder.

Click the Search button and Windows Media Player will run a system scan, looking for compatible music files on the drives and in the folders specified in Steps 4 and 5. Each file it finds will be catalogued in the Media Library and will thereafter be accessible from within Media Center.

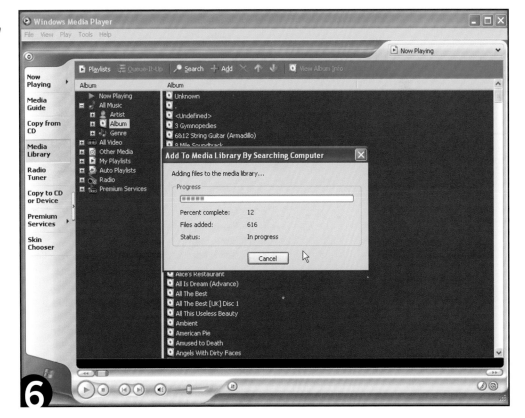

To ensure that Windows Media Player automatically detects and identifies new music files whenever they are added to My Music or any other folder, set up folder monitoring. Still in the Media Library section of Windows Media Player, click the Add button and select By Monitoring Folders. Now click the Add button and navigate to any folder that contains music files, be it local (i.e. on the Media Center) or remote (i.e. on a networked computer). Add each in turn. You don't need to do anything else: from now, any files added to or removed from monitored folders will show up in Media Center's My Music module.

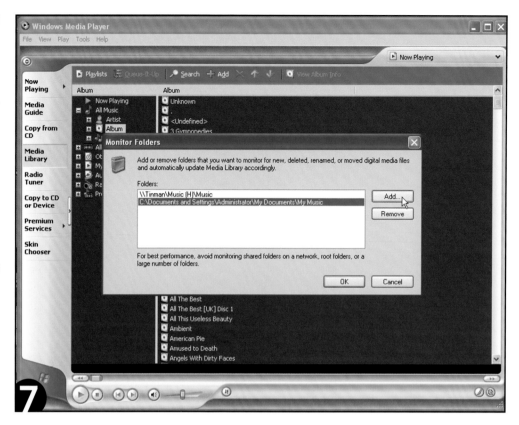

Exploring My Music

The effectiveness of the My Music module hinges upon how accurately your MP3 and WMA files are labelled with artist, album, track and genre information. This data is held in ID3 'tags'. If a track doesn't contain album information in its ID3 tag, it won't appear as an album track to Media Center. Likewise, you'll find an album entry for every track tagged as an album track even if it is the only track you have from that album. Contrariwise, you may find that albums are incomplete even when you know that you have all the requisite tracks: if some of its tracks are incorrectly tagged, or not tagged at all, Media Center simply doesn't 'know' that they belong to a specific album and you won't find them where you expect to.

Importantly, albums in Media Center do not necessarily reflect your music folders. For instance, you might have a folder on your hard drive called My Fave Pop Hits that contains a dozen disparate MP3 tracks. You may even be used to thinking of this folder as an 'album' when you play music on your computer. To Media Center, though, the folder is irrelevant. All it cares, or rather knows, about is how each track in that folder identifies itself with its ID3 tag.

All that aside for a moment, let's dive in. Once Windows Media Player has been configured, launch Media Center and open My Music. From the main menu, you have seven options. Here is a quick run-through of the main features.

In this example, Media Center reports an album called Bitches Brew. However, it appears to contains but a single track. The other tracks may well exist on the Media Center PC somewhere but unless they are tagged with the same album and artist information as this track, Media Center won't treat them as being related.

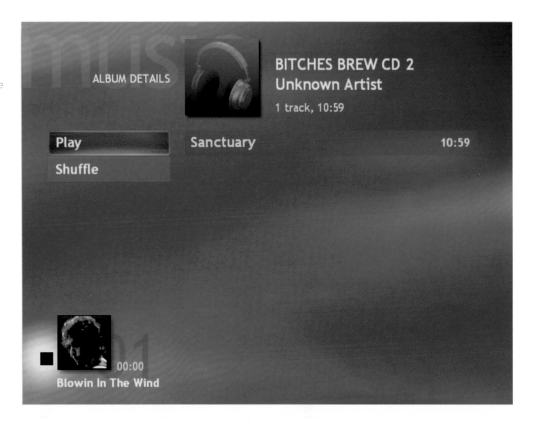

The My Music menu is the launchpad for finding, sorting and playing music, whether MP3/WMA tracks stored on the hard disk drive or audio CDs. Albums view is the default entry point.

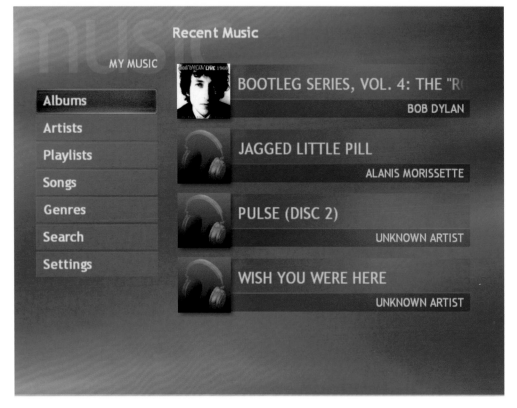

Select Albums from the My Music menu to see a list of all albums catalogued behind the scenes by the Windows Media Player Media Library. View it either as a simple list of titles or as large icons with pictures of album covers (where available). On the latter point, this is the feature whereby Media Center downloads information, including artwork, to display alongside your music if you gave it permission to do so during setup (see Step 1 on p.99).

Use the arrow or Channel/Page buttons to scroll through your albums. Highlight an album, press Play and you should hear the first track. A new Now Playing window shows you all tracks on that album. Scroll through to select and play an alternative track. Otherwise, if left alone, the entire album will play in sequence.

During playback, you can use the transport controls on your remote just as if you were using a CD player. Play, Stop and Pause all do what you expect; the Skip button jumps to the next track; Replay jumps back to the previous track; and Fast Forward speeds up playback (note that Rewind does not work with MP3/WMA files).

If you highlight an album from the Album screen and press OK, you can view its track list. Now use the Play menu option to play all tracks in the order in which they are shown, select Shuffle to play them in a random order, or select an individual track to play it alone. Note that any currently playing music continues to play in the preview window until you make a new selection.

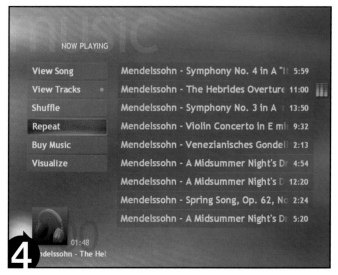

While an album is playing, you have some new options in the Now Playing screen. View Song shows you information about the currently playing track while View Tracks returns you to the full track listing. Shuffle shuffles track order and Repeat repeats the entire album. Buy Music you can (and should, we suggest) ignore.

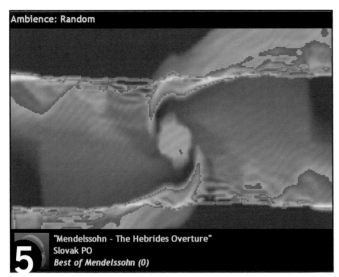

The Visualise option fills your screen with swirling patterns intended to complement the music. This can be remarkably effective on a large TV screen. Use the left/right arrow buttons on your remote to switch from one visualisation to another and the Back button to return to the Now Playing screen.

From the main My Music menu, select Artists. This shows you music sorted alphabetically by artist name, again using information held in file ID3 tags. Scroll through the list until you find an artist that you want to hear, then highlight the name and press OK to see full album and track listings. Don't be surprised to find multiple entries in the Artists view: ID3 information is often misspelled or a simple typo is enough to throw Media Center off track. Here we see three versions of one artist and two of another. Again, see Appendix 2 for more on ID3 tags.

Back to My Music and select Playlists. A playlist is a collection of tracks pre-configured to play consecutively, regardless of source. Tracks may come from the same album or folder, but may just as easily be stored on different drives or computers. The computer doesn't care: it simply plays them in the order specified by the playlist. Unfortunately, you cannot create playlists in Media Center but must instead revert to Windows Media Player – a serious drawback.

To be fair, Media Center has a stab at making its own playlists based on criteria like tracks you play most or least often, those you tend to listen to during the day, evening or weekend, those recorded with the highest and lowest quality settings, and so forth. Perhaps the most useful approach is creating an Auto Playlist exclusively from 4- and 5-star rated tracks, as this way you stand a good chance of hearing only music that you particularly like. Or at least you would do if it was possible to give tracks star ratings with Media Center. Once again, sadly, this is the territory of Windows Media Player and Appendix 2.

9 The Songs menu option provides an alphabetical list of each and every music track listed in the Media Library. Use the Channel/Page button to scroll through a screen at a time.

10 If you'd like to see what you have in the way of Folk, Funk or Fusion, Media Center can sort your collection into the appropriate genres. Needless to say, this works only for tracks that have ID3 tags, and then only when the information is 'correct' (there's always room for interpretation here, particularly with music that resists narrow pigeon-holing).

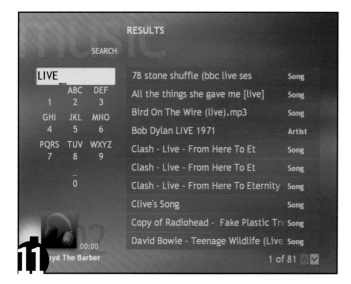

11 The Search option works just like the Programme Guide search feature discussed on p.94: tap in a word or a few letters and Media Center serves up music tracks that contain those terms in the track title or artist name. Basic but effective.

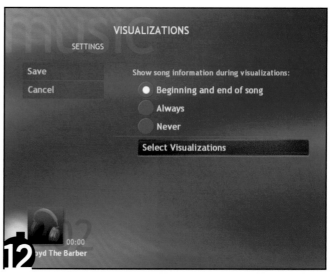

12 The Settings button leads to a simple screen that lets you determine how, and if, track information is displayed during those psychedelic visualisations mentioned in Step 5. If you'd prefer an unbroken picture show, select Never. You can also turn specific visualisations on and off here, which might conceivably be useful if you prefer the Alchemy style to Plenoptic, whatever they may be.

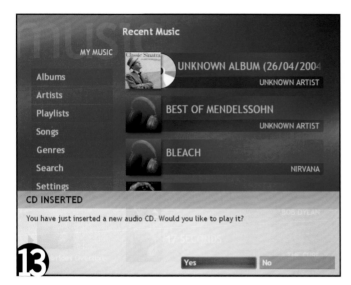

13 *Pop a CD in the computer drive (either drive if it has two) and Media Center will play it. It doesn't get much simpler than that.*

14 *If the PC is currently online and if you gave it permission to retrieve information from the internet, Media Center will attempt to discover the CD title, artist and track listing from an online database. Success is not guaranteed (but if it fails, see Appendix 2).*

So long as the CD remains in the drive, the album shows up in My Music's Albums, Artists, Genre and other sections. The moment you remove the CD, it disappears from the Media Library; next time you put it back in, Media Center recognises the disc and uses the same information.

But why bother using CDs at all, at least more than once? During playback, you'll see an additional option in the Now Playing screen: Copy CD. Select this now.

The first thing you must do is decide whether or not to add copy protection to your 'rip'. Without getting into a debate about the pros and cons of 'digital rights management', it's much simpler to say no. You won't be asked this again.

The following Copy Options screen suggests some alternative recording formats. Media Center will record using the WMA file format and a constant bit rate of 128Kbps. You can improve the quality of the recording by upping this to 192Kbps, variable bit rate or 'lossless' recording – see Step 3 on p.100 – but only by reverting to the Windows Media Player programme and changing the defaults. You won't see this screen again either: from now on, Media Center will use the default recording settings without further question.

When you click Finish, Media Center will copy the CD to the hard disk drive. From now on, you can play this album directly from the computer without needing the CD. It will, however, look like the same album to My Music because Media Center makes no distinction between CDs and digital audio files.

15

PART  My Pictures

A Media Center PC connected to a television set provides an excellent platform for showcasing digital images, be they stills from a digital camera or scans of traditional film prints. You may find it easier, more fun and certainly more economical to gather the family around the TV for a post-holiday slideshow than to print off hard copies. Again, you can include images held on a different computer on a network without having to copy them across to the Media Center.

File locations

Media Center can find and 'play' pictures providing they are stored in one of three locations. First, the My Pictures folder, which is a sub-folder of My Documents (just like My Music). Any supported image files saved here or in any sub-folder within My Pictures can be viewed.

Secondly, Media Center looks to the Shared Pictures folder, which is a sub-folder of Shared Documents. This is useful primarily if you have a number of user accounts set up on your Windows XP computer, something that we're not concerned with here. The default location of this folder, should you need to navigate to it manually, is C:/Documents and Settings/All Users/Documents/Shared Pictures.

Thirdly, Media Center can read images directly from a memory card, assuming that the computer is equipped with a memory card reader, or from a CD containing images.

In addition, Media Center can read pictures in any folder, either on its own hard disk drive or on a networked computer, providing that you place a shortcut to that folder in either the My Pictures or Shared Pictures folders. This requires working in Windows.

My Pictures supports several common image file formats, notably JPG, TIF, GIF and BMP. If you have images in a different format, convert them to a supported format using any image editing application.

Here, with My Pictures selected in the menu on the left, we can see that there are two available images. Others may be held in Shared Pictures or Other media.

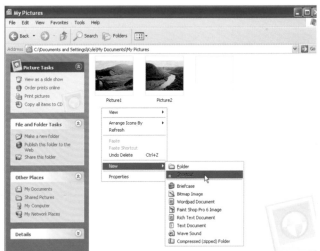

In Windows, open the My Pictures or Shared Pictures folders, right-click a clear spot, select New > Shortcut, and navigate to any local or shared remote folder that contains images you want to display in Media Center.

Exploring My Pictures

In the following steps, we run through the full gamut of My Pictures' capabilities.

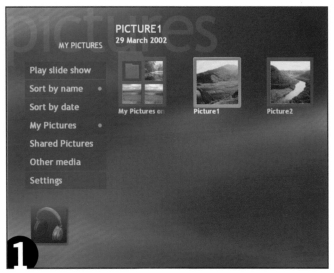

Open My Pictures with the button on your Media Center remote. From the menu on the left, select either My Pictures or Shared Pictures; or, if you have a memory card currently in the computer's memory card reader or a CD containing images in the CD or DVD drive, Other media. Each individual, or loose, image within that folder is displayed as a thumbnail and each sub-folder as an icon that bears mini-thumbnails of images held within it. Use the arrow or Channel/Page buttons to move around the thumbnails and highlight any image. Press OK.

The selected image will now be displayed full screen. Use the left/right arrow buttons to display the previous/next images in the folder, thereby viewing them all in turn. You can also press the Play button to initiate a slideshow. All images in the same folder as that image will then be displayed sequentially according the options determined in the Settings menu (see Step 10 below). By default, Media Center applies a little animated panning and scanning to liven up the show. Use the left and right arrow keys to hop backwards and forwards between pictures during a slideshow, or the Pause button to temporarily halt playback.

3

Use the Back button to return to the My Pictures menu. Now highlight a folder or folder shortcut from the thumbnail menu. Press OK to open that folder and its contents will be displayed in thumbnail mode. Again, it may contain loose images and further folders.

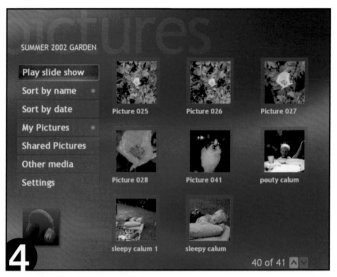

4

Highlight any folder or folder shortcut and press the Play button on your remote. All images within that folder will be displayed in a slideshow. Alternatively, select the Play slide show option from the on-screen menu at any time. The contents of whichever folder is currently open in thumbnail view will be played in a slideshow, including pictures within sub-folders (but see Step 10).

5

Whenever an image is in full-screen display mode, press the OK button once to zoom in on it, and again to zoom in some more. While thus zoomed, use the arrow keys to pan around the image. Press OK a third time to return the image to normal size, followed by Back to return to a thumbnail menu.

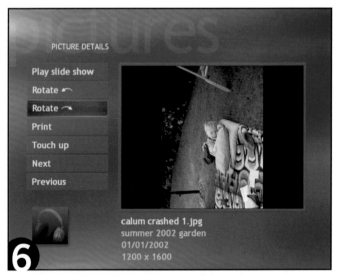

6

Highlight any image thumbnail and press the More Info button (or press More Info while an image is on full-screen display). Up pops a new Picture Details screen with a bunch of choices. Helpfully, you can rotate images by 90-degree in either direction if they need straightening. To do this, highlight one or other of the Rotate keys and press OK once (90-degree rotation) or twice (180-degrees) until the picture is displayed in the correct orientation.

7

8

The Print button in the Picture Details screen is obvious: select this and the current image will be printed full-page on your default printer. Slightly less obvious are the Touch Up tools. The Contrast button seeks to make pictures clearer; and the Red eye button attempts to automatically remove camera-flash-induced red eye. We have found these tools to be disappointing and surprisingly effective respectively. They are certainly no substitute for a proper image editing application if your pictures need serious enhancement. Select the Save button to make any change permanent. This alters the original file and is not available if the file is stored on read-only media or on a network location where you have read-only 'rights'.

You can play music during a slideshow but Media Center's implementation of this feature is clunky in the extreme. Essentially, you have to fire up My Music first, select a track or album, and commence playback. Then return to My Pictures and start a slideshow. During the show, you can use the Skip and Replay buttons to jump between tracks. The Pause button pauses both the slideshow and the soundtrack, and Stop stops them both. Track information is displayed in an information bar at the start of each fresh track, unless you turn this option off in the Settings menu (see Step 9).

9

10

Back in the main My Pictures menu, select the Settings buttons. Options here relate to the slideshow feature and let you determine whether or not pictures are shown with transitions ('animated' means the default pan and scan effect – turn this off if you prefer to view static images during a slideshow); the transition time (how long each picture stays on screen); and how, or if, soundtrack information is displayed.

The important option here is Show pictures in subfolders. If this is checked, as it is by default, then a slideshow will include all images within a selected folder, whether they are loose or stored in separate sub-folders. In Step 1, for instance, a default slideshow would display Picture 1 and Picture 2 plus the entire contents of the folder shortcut, including any further hidden sub-folders. If you uncheck the option, the slideshow would comprise Picture 1 and Picture 2 only, i.e. only loose images are included. Remember to save any changes before leaving this screen.

PART 4 Play DVD and My Videos

There's really not a great deal to say here. Media Center plays DVDs and videos in full-screen mode, effectively replacing the standard standalone DVD player in your living room. It's just as easy to use and, because it can play video files stored on a hard disk drive as easily as DVD movies, a good deal more flexible.

Playing a DVD

Pop a DVD movie in the DVD drive and Media Center will offer to play it immediately. If you set up the parental controls option back on p.66, you may need to enter your 4-digit code at this point.

The transport buttons on your remote (see pp.52–53) let you pause, speed up, slow down and otherwise control playback. Use the Skip and Replay buttons to jump between chapters – pre-marked points in the movie – and the More Info button to see at a glance which chapter you're currently watching. The volume button controls volume, the Stop button stops playback, and so forth. Your remote also has a special DVD Menu button that takes you straight to the DVD disc's main menu wherein you can access special features, browse chapters (usually called scene selections), set languages, turn on subtitles and explore whatever else the publisher included on the disc.

Media Center is set up by default to auto-play CDs and DVDs. This means that a movie is ready to play with a minimum of fuss.

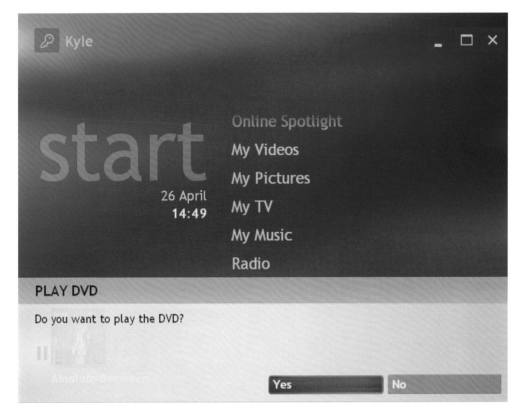

Use the remote to control DVD and video playback as if you were using a standalone DVD player.

Sort out your speaker settings here. It is possible to navigate menus like this with the remote buttons, but a mouse makes it easier.

It's really as simple as that, although it is worthwhile checking one setting. Press the Green start button, select Settings, and select DVD. Now select the Audio button and ensure that the computer knows how many speakers you have and how they are connected (the precise appearance of this screen depends on the DVD-decoding software installed on your PC). Here, because we are using an optical digital output, we can select SPDIF (Sony/Philips Digital Interface).

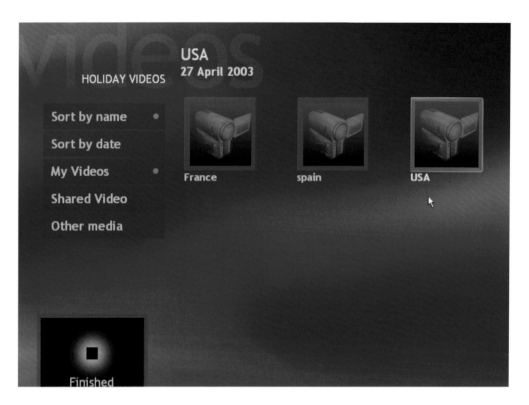

From the main Media Center menu, select My Videos. Any clips stored in one of the two key folders or linked to with a shortcut show up as clickable icons. Select a clip to play it.

HOLIDAY VIDEOS

USA
27 April 2003

Sort by name

Sort by date

My Videos

Shared Video

Other media

France   spain   USA

Finished

Working with videos

Media Center can play video clips stored locally on the hard disk drive, remotely on a networked computer, or directly from a CD or DVD disc. You can even connect a digital camcorder and access its footage through the Other media option.

File locations works in a similar manner to the My Pictures module. Media Center will find video files only if they are located in two key folders – My Videos (a sub-folder of My Documents) and Shared Videos (a sub-folder of Shared Documents) – or if either of these folders contains a shortcut to another folder. Shortcuts can point to local folders (on the same computer) or remote folders (on a networked computer). However, do be warned that you are unlikely to be able to successfully stream video clips over a wireless network unless you have one of the newer, higher-bandwidth Wi-Fi standards (IEEE 802.11a or g). Even then, playback may be flaky.

In fact, the Media Center My Videos module is really just a pretty interface for Windows Media Player, the muscle behind movie (and music) playback. What this means in practice is that Media Center can play any video files that Windows Media Player can play – and none of those that it can't. The snag is that many clips distributed on the internet use codecs that Windows Media Player does not natively support (a codec is a compression/decompression software technique that reduces

video file sizes). Thus you may download the latest funny clip only to find that you can't play it in My Videos. Worse, the computer may hang and require a reboot.

One solution is downloading and installing new codecs as and when required, but this means working in the Windows environment. Alternatively, only play video files that you know Media Center can handle. Supported file formats include MPEG-1 and -2, AVI, WMV and ASF (although even here specialist codecs can render a file unplayable: the popular DivX codec, for example, produces highly-compressed AVI files that Media Center cannot handle without a codec upgrade).

If you are a home movie enthusiast, you can of course capture, edit and produce your videos on the Media Center computer, using Windows XP's own Movie Maker 2 application or any other program of your choice. Movie Maker 2 uses a file format called Windows Media Video that Media Center fully supports. Once you have produced and saved a home movie, Media Center will play it as if it was playing a DVD.

However, do be aware that Media Center itself is only the showcase for your efforts: the grunt work, from connecting a camera to capturing video to editing, producing and saving the final movie, requires working in Windows XP – and that, as we know, means using a mouse, keyboard and monitor.

No suitable codec means no video playback.

Movie Maker 2 is a digital video editor bundled with Windows XP.

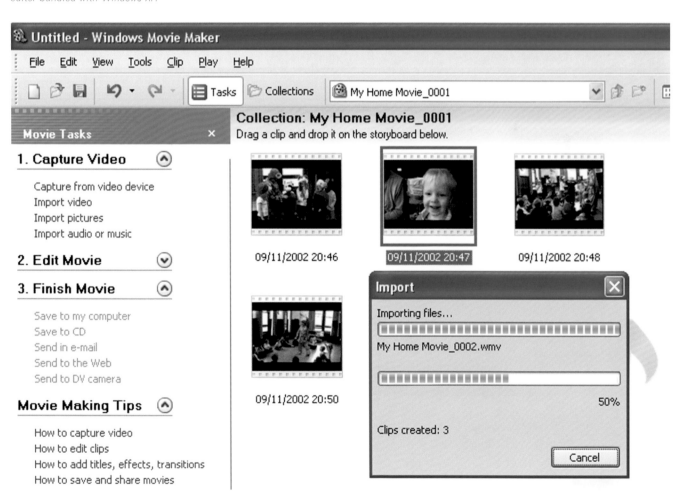

PART  Radio and Online Spotlight

If your Media Center computer has an FM radio tuner installed, you can use the Radio module to listen to, pause, replay and record radio stations in virtually the same way that you can watch, pause and record live TV in My TV. If it doesn't, you can't.

Or, if your television service includes digital radio stations, you can use My TV itself to record stations. These should be listed alongside TV channels in the Guide, with (or sometimes without) schedule and programme information.

If you have an always-on broadband internet connection, there's another option courtesy of Online Spotlight, one of the options listed in the main Media Center menu. Quite what you see in here will vary over time, but you should certainly find a link to dozens, perhaps even hundreds, of online radio stations, all searchable by genre or title and all completely free. Hone in on the Music section and explore.

When you find a station that you like, use the Add to My Radio link. Media Center will ask if it's OK to download a small file. Agree to this.

From now on, that station and any others you add will appear as entries in the Media Center Radio module. You can tune in directly from here.

One thing you can't do with Media Center is record music from online stations, although you can buffer and pause a live stream.

Elsewhere in Online Spotlight, you will find Media Center tips and tricks, program updates and enhancements, and doubtless some special offers on software. One that's certainly worth checking out is Sonic PrimeTime, as this is one of the (as yet) few programs currently able to burn TV shows recorded in Media Center to DVD (see Appendix 1). Unfortunately, Online Spotlight options have a habit of firing up standard web pages that look lousy on a TV screen, particularly where downloads are required. The radio service provided by Live365.com is an honourable exception.

Tune in to your favourite stations manually.

This, we fear, is a common state of affairs with Media Centers.

Even Freeview throws in a good selection of digital radio stations.

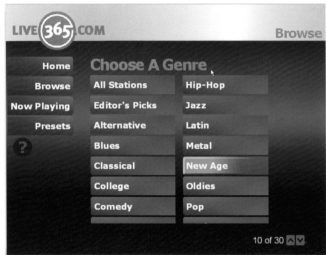

More music than you can handle, conveniently sorted by genre (and paid for by advertising).

Like what you hear? Add the station to your personal collection.

'Saved' stations are accessible from the Radio module without having to go through Online Spotlight again. Remember that you have to be online to hear them.

One day, hopefully, all Online Spotlight services will be designed for the Media Center interface. Not yet, though.

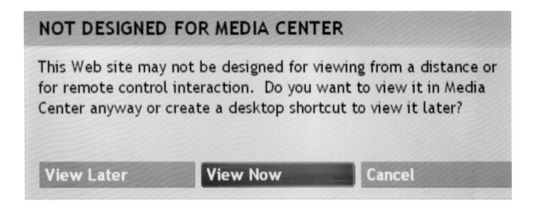

NOT DESIGNED FOR MEDIA CENTER

This Web site may not be designed for viewing from a distance or for remote control interaction. Do you want to view it in Media Center anyway or create a desktop shortcut to view it later?

View Later   View Now   Cancel

PART 5 The DIY alternative

PART ⑤ **Building or customising a computer**

Not for the first time, we wish to emphasise that Microsoft Media Center Edition 2004 is an application, not a device. It's really little more than a pretty interface that sits on top of Windows XP, can be controlled with a remote control and provides home entertainment functionality that mimics that of consumer electronics hardware. By and large, Media Center is a highly effective implementation of intuitive and powerful software. However, with the exception of the Programme Guide, it is perfectly possible to achieve much the same end without Media Center software.

The ABC of DIY

Any adequately equipped computer, particularly a powerful Windows XP model, can turn its hand to home entertainment. Cast a glance back to pp.28–30 for a summary of the stipulated Media Center hardware. If your PC already matches those requirements, or if you're prepared to give it an update in key areas, it's probably not so far away. In fact, you may already use it for playing audio CDs and MP3 files, and perhaps for DVDs, too. You might use it to edit, sort and display digital images, and perhaps for playing video clips. You've probably discovered

internet radio, and you may even play PC games (games-playing is not one of Media Center's strengths, which is why we ignore it in this manual). If it has a TV tuner card, it's even possible that you watch and record live television on your computer.

The downside is that you have to use different software programs for these tasks, with nothing holding it all together in a unified Media Center-style interface. But that's something we can change.

More importantly, we'll bet that your computer isn't permanently connected to the TV. That's where Media Center

It's possible to connect just about any PC to a TV, whether or not it has a dedicated TV-out port (S-Video or composite video), but you'll have to use the monitor port. This means that you can't keep a monitor and TV connected simultaneously. Here's a device that converts a VGA monitor port to S-Video with the help of USB.

scores serious points: to be an integrated home entertainment hub, it must migrate from the study to the living room. Would you give your current whirring, wheezing, beige, ugly desktop-style PC similar house room? Unlikely. Besides, without the Media Center interface, you would have to control it with a mouse and keyboard, and there's no fun in that. Nor, as we've said, can you buy Media Center in a box and install it on your Windows XP computer. It is only available pre-installed on new computers and new Media Center computers cost a pretty penny.

This section, then, is for those of you who would like to own a Media Center-like computer but have no intention of buying one off the shelf. We'll look first, albeit briefly, at how to build one from scratch (see the Haynes *Build Your Own Computer* manual for a full step-by-step guide); and then look in more detail at alternative software that turns any customised computer into something very similar to a Media Center – including, crucially, the inclusion of an Electronic Programme Guide for PVR functionality.

Small is beautiful

Well, less ugly, at least. The trend towards hardware miniaturisation continues unabated these days, and a whole new generation of 'bare bones' micro-computers is available. The beauty of this approach is threefold. First, you buy the essentials – a case, power supply and motherboard – in kit form and then choose the other components – processor, memory, drives and expansion cards – yourself. This means that you can effectively build a custom computer that precisely meets your home entertainment requirements. Secondly, if you choose wisely, you'll find that the motherboard provides all you need in the way of sound, graphics and connectivity, which means you don't have to bother with sound cards, video cards, network interface cards and all the rest. Integration at source is the key and very welcome it is too when space is tight. Which brings us to the final point: these new bare-bones kits are sleek, smart and very, very small, designed specifically to save space and look good tucked under the TV. They are also whisper-quiet. Here's a look at the Zen Shuttle bare-bones systems.

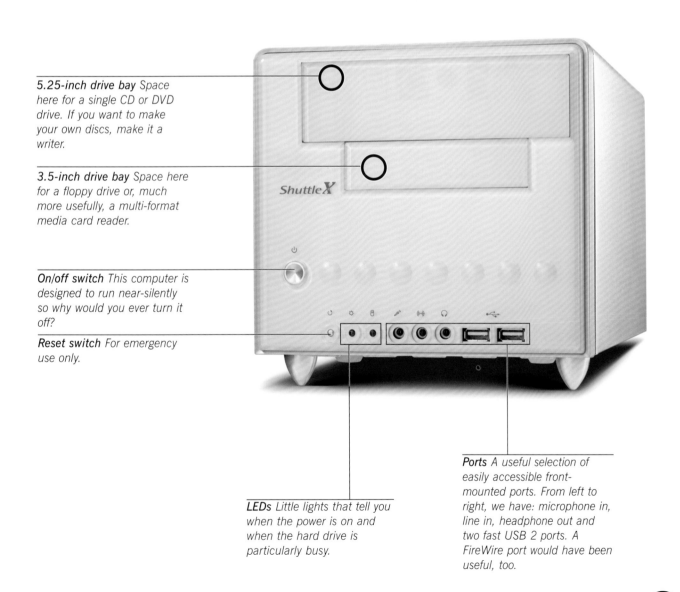

5.25-inch drive bay *Space here for a single CD or DVD drive. If you want to make your own discs, make it a writer.*

3.5-inch drive bay *Space here for a floppy drive or, much more usefully, a multi-format media card reader.*

On/off switch *This computer is designed to run near-silently so why would you ever turn it off?*

Reset switch *For emergency use only.*

LEDs *Little lights that tell you when the power is on and when the hard drive is particularly busy.*

Ports *A useful selection of easily accessible front-mounted ports. From left to right, we have: microphone in, line in, headphone out and two fast USB 2 ports. A FireWire port would have been useful, too.*

Optical audio in (SPDIF) Connect any other device that has an optical audio output here.

Fan grill Essential internal ventilation.

Expansion card cover There's room for just one expansion card here but with sound, high-quality (i.e. AGP) graphics and networking all provided by the motherboard, this should be sufficient. For our home entertainment project, we'll be plugging in a TV tuner card.

VGA A standard analogue monitor port.

Power connector To save space, reduce noise and cut down on cooling, this computer kit comes with an external power supply. It plugs in here.

Optical audio out (SPDIF) The easy way to feed a multi-channel speaker setup.

Audio Three audio ports that together can pump surround sound to a compatible speaker system. You could use just the green port to feed stereo speakers, including those in your TV.

Clear CMOS An unusual button that lets you reset the motherboard's CMOS (Complimentary Metal Oxide Semiconductor). This is a form of permanent memory that tells the device about itself upon every reboot.

Serial A 'legacy' interface that could conceivably be useful for connecting an ancient modem.

Mouse and keyboard sockets

S-Video Ideal for connecting a television set. If your computer has a standard video card, it may not include an S-Video (or composite video) output, in which case you're going to struggle to wire up the PC to a TV. A video card upgrade would be warranted. In this case, you should certainly consider one of the all-in-one video cards that have built-in TV tuners. ATI is the best known manufacturer of such cards.

IEEE 1394 (FireWire) A pair of these, perfect for connecting digital camcorders and external hard drives.

USB 2 Another pair of USB ports.

Ethernet Built-in networking.

Easy steps to a custom computer

As just mentioned, the attraction of a bare-bones kit is that you start off with the essentials and then add extras to suit. Here we'll quickly run through a representative assembly process. If you've never attempted such a thing before, be assured that it's remarkably straightforward. Here we're using the Shuttle Zen kit shown on the previous pages.

Lift the lid. As it is held on with three thumbscrews, this is a simple procedure. We should at this juncture mention the standard safety precautions: never work with live electricity (i.e. unplug everything before you begin); give yourself adequate space, light and time to work comfortably; read and follow the manufacturer's manual; and ideally wear an antistatic wrist-strap and work on an antistatic mat to protect delicate computer components from electrostatic discharge.

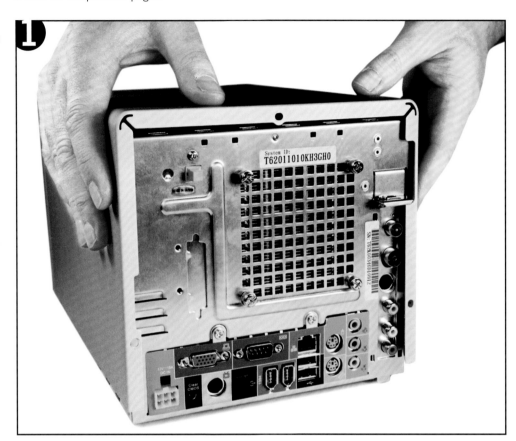

Having disassembled the kit if it arrived partially preassembled, pop in a processor and lock it in place in its socket. Unless you're planning to use this computer as a fully-fledged office machine, there's no need to break the budget. The vital thing is to ensure that you buy a make and model supported by the motherboard. The motherboard or computer kit manual will make this clear.

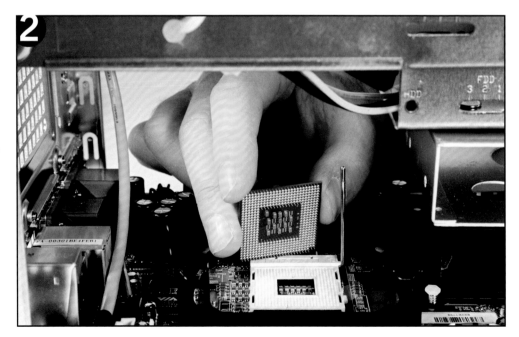

Processors must be cooled, and this means bolting on a heatsink to dissipate heat. To ensure a good bond between the processor and the heatsink, you need either thermal interface glue, as shown here, or a thermal pad stuck on the base of the heatsink. If using glue, spread it out evenly over the surface of the processor.

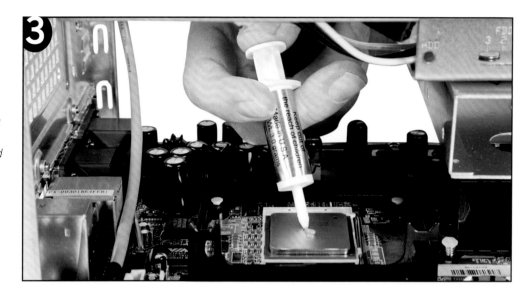

Carefully lower the heatsink unit onto the processor. It will be designed to fit one way around only in a frame that surrounds the processor. In 'normal' computers, the heatsink usually has a fan affixed but here cool air will be blown to the processor through a series of pipes from a fan affixed to the rear ventilation grill. It's a clever and effective arrangement that reduces noise and makes the computer more acceptable in a domestic setting. Handle with care.

The heatsink must now be secured in position by clamping it to the processor socket. This requires a bit of force. Try to get it right first time around, as you really don't want to overly disturb the thermal material between the processor and the heatsink. Space is tight so it's all a little awkward.

In this overhead shot, we can see the cooling pipes running vertically to the heatsink from the fan, which is itself encased in a protective grill and in position to be attached to the case (Step 8).

Very importantly, locate the fan power connector on the motherboard and plug in the fan's power cable. Here, the cable has three wires – red, yellow and black – and plugs in between the processor socket and the expansion card slot

Screw the fan securely in place. Again, this design uses thumbscrews, which means you don't even need a screwdriver. The processor is now in place, protected by a heatsink which will be cooled by the fan sucking in cool air from outside the case.

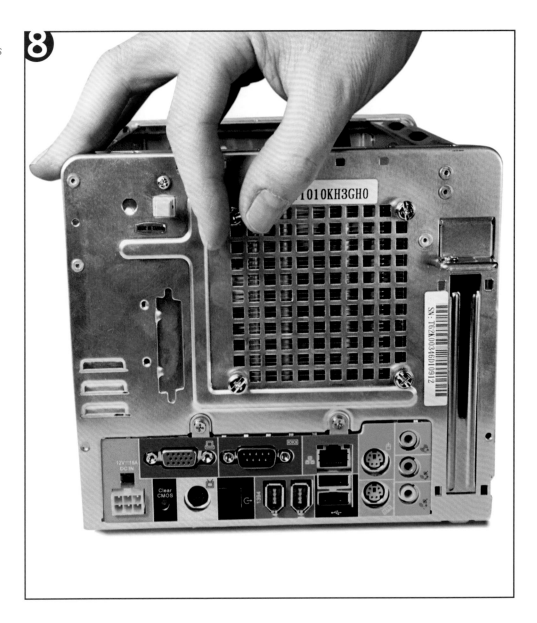

Slot in a compatible RAM (memory) module. This design has two slots for memory and supports up to a maximum 2GB of memory. We were satisfied with a single 256MB module. Like the processor, it is essential to source only memory that is fully compatible with the motherboard.

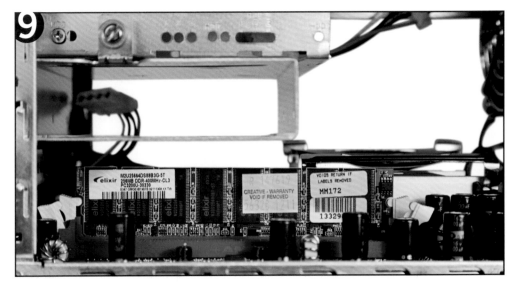

The hard drive gets attached with four screws to a removable caddy that then slides neatly into a drive bay and is secured by means of a single spring-loaded thumbscrew. It's all very ingenious and makes the most of limited internal space.

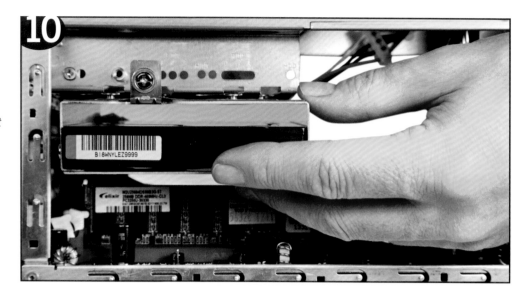

Around the other side now, connect the hard disk drive's power and data cables. The power cable (four wires connected to a white plug) has been routed through channels in the case to prevent the risk of impeding airflow – another cracking design feature – and the data cable (black, wide, supplied with the kit) is just long enough to stretch to the drive from the socket on the motherboard.

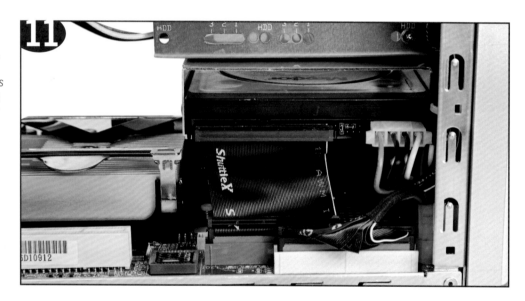

Here we have installed a TV tuner card in the motherboard's one available PCI expansion slot. You could choose a digital model if you want to pick up Freeview channels or an analogue card if you intend to hook up a cable, satellite or Freeview set-top box (refer back to pp.28–29 & 39 for more on all this). Or, of course, you could use an external TV tuner (see p.131 for an example) and use the slot for a different purpose: a modem, perhaps, if you are unable to access the internet via the built-in network port.

You need to install a drive to play CDs and DVDs and, optionally, to make your own. If you are going to connect your new home entertainment computer to a network and you already have a writer drive installed in a different computer, you might choose to transfer files across the network for burning rather than duplicating hardware unnecessarily. That's why we plumped for a basic DVD-ROM drive here. Drives screw into place in a standard drive bay. Now is the time to install a media card reader alongside it, if so desired.

Now we loaded Windows XP, hooked the PC up to a decent sound system, connected it via S-Video to the television set, plugged it into an existing home network (with internet sharing on tap), and prepared to make merry with our new home entertainment centre. You can do the same or something very similar. Bearing in mind all that has gone before, it would be nice to install the Media Center software, but that is not an option. Instead, we had to find an alternative.

PART

Getting ready for ShowShifter

On the following pages, we look at what is probably the best known (and arguably the best) of the alternatives to Media Center software: ShowShifter, from a company called Home Media Networks.

ShowShifter is reasonably priced, with the exact cost depending on whether you opt for the Standard or Pro version, and whether you intend to use it with an analogue or digital TV card. However, the software is entirely free to use for the first fifteen days, so you can install it and try it thoroughly before parting with any cash. During this period, none of its features are restricted or disabled.

What does ShowShifter offer?

ShowShifter provides pretty much the same set of features as a Media Center PC. It takes all the existing tools your PC has for

playing CDs and DVDs, managing music, watching videos and displaying digital images, and wraps them all up in a highly-visible point-and-click interface you can control from a distance using a wireless mouse or handheld remote.

It also adds a TiVo-like facility for watching TV and recording it to hard disk drive, complete with a time-shifting function that lets you pause a live TV broadcast and resume watching it from the

ShowShifter showcases digital images just as effectively as Media Center's My Pictures module.

Unlike a cumbersome printed programme guide, the electronic version in ShowShifter can search for programmes based on subject matter and key words.

same point after a break. On top of this, it provides a completely free Electronic Programme Guide (no subscription required) to help when planning your viewing and to make setting timer recordings foolproof.

Will ShowShifter work on your PC?

You probably already own all the supporting software required by ShowShifter. Top of the list is Windows Media Player 9 which, with the support of a software ally called DirectX 9, copes with most types of media. Apart from TV, that is: video recording in ShowShifter is performed courtesy of the free DivX codec. This is

incorporated in the ShowShifter download and is automatically installed alongside it.

The only stumbling block is that, like Windows itself, ShowShifter cannot play DVD/MPEG-2 movies unless a suitable external codec is installed. The necessary codec is automatically added to Windows when you install commercial DVD software players such as WinDVD and PowerDVD, and the chances are that one of these programs was supplied with your PC or with its DVD drive. If not, you'll need to get hold of one.

In hardware terms, the only special tool you need is a TV tuner. The cheaper ones are very inexpensive and they're readily

ShowShifter's Jukebox uses the same audio codecs and visualisations as Windows Media Player.

If your PC can play DVDs using a program like PowerDVD, then it can also play them from within ShowShifter.

available from the usual PC outlets and superstores. Most people plump for one of Hauppauge's internal or external devices (available in analogue and digital versions) or for an all-in-one graphics card and tuner like those from ATI. Note that an all-in-one card is not usually an option if you build your own PC along the lines described earlier, as such cards require AGP slots. To save space, micro-PCs (like the one we've just been working with) provide AGP graphics output by means of a chip soldered on the motherboard, so no slot is provided.

A digital tuner will deliver better pictures and a wider choice of channels, providing digital broadcasting reception is adequate in

your area (check this at **www.freeview.co.uk**).

You can also feed a video signal to an analogue tuner from a cable, satellite or Freeview set-top box. However, unlike Media Center, you won't be able to change channels on the STB. There is a workaround of sorts if you buy an approved IR transmitter — see **www.showshifter.com/support/irtrans.htm** for details, such as they are, which is scant – but otherwise you'll have to use your STB's own remote control whenever you want to change channel. In our non-geek view, this is a major drawback, if not a fatal flaw. We believe that ShowShifter is best suited to working with either an analogue tuner that picks up the five standard

An external TV tuner is a convenient way of bringing TV to your computer without requiring surgery (even if we are being a touch optimistic with the portable aerial). Note the Marmitek remote control here. We'll talk about this on p.149.

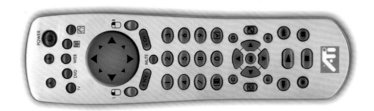

If your TV tuner card comes with a remote control, you can program it to control ShowShifter (see pp.147–149).

terrestrial channels or, better, a digital tuner that brings you Freeview.

You don't need a remote control to operate ShowShifter, but having one adds greatly to the convenience of using the program. The cheapest way to get hold of a remote is by choosing a TV tuner that comes bundled with one in the box (including, of course, the required infrared receiver). Any type of IR remote with at least six buttons will do.

Back up and be safe

ShowShifter won't turn your PC into a Media Center clone because the ShowShifter interface and modes of operation are entirely original. What it will do is provide virtually identical

features on a standard or custom-built PC at minimal cost. In fact, if you already have a TV card, it will cost you nothing to try ShowShifter for 15 days.

However, it is not advisable to install and use ShowShifter without first making a backup of your hard disk drive, or at the very least setting a System Restore point before installation. This is especially true if you already use the DivX video codec because ShowShifter's settings will override the existing configuration.

Checking specs and getting going

Before ploughing ahead and installing ShowShifter, check that your computer is up to the job and ready to take it on-board.

The minimum hardware requirements to run ShowShifter are an 800MHz Pentium III or equivalent processor, 64MB of RAM and 300MB of free hard disk drive space. But these are very much the base line and a more realistic specification for good performance is a 2GHz processor, 256MB of RAM and upwards of 30GB of free hard disk drive space for storing TV recordings. The more space you have, the more programmes you can record, and the higher the recorded quality. You also need a sound card compatible with DirectX (it's hard to find one that isn't) and a graphics card that can support 32-bit colour. To check this, right-click anywhere on the Windows Desktop and select Properties from the menu. Open the Settings tab and check that the setting in the Color Quality panel reads Highest (32 bit). Change it if necessary. If 32 bit is not one of the available options, you may need an updated graphics driver or an updated graphics card. The latter is unlikely unless your PC is several years old.

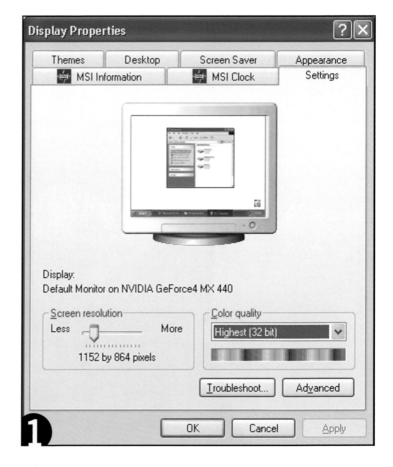

ShowShifter will run on all versions of Windows from Windows 98 onwards, but works best with Windows 2000 or XP. What is really important is having the latest version of DirectX. At the time of writing, this is version 9.0b. To find out which version you have, click Start, then Run, and type dxdiag into the Run box. When you click OK, the DirectX Diagnostic Tool starts up (if it doesn't then you definitely need to install a new copy of DirectX!). The last line of system information on the opening screen tells you which version is currently installed. You can download the latest version from **www.microsoft.com/windows/directx**.

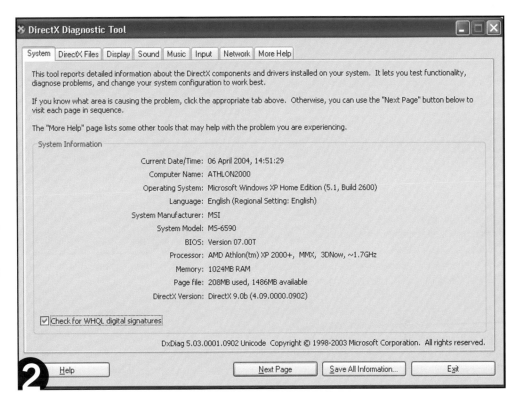

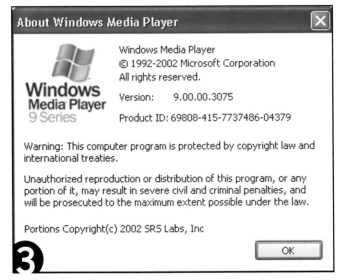

Although ShowShifter works with any version of Windows Media Player from 7.1 onwards, for optimum performance and additional features you should install Windows Media Player Series 9. To see which version you've got, start Media Player, click on Help, and select About Windows Media Player. The latest version, if you need it, can be downloaded from **www.microsoft.com/windows/windowsmedia**.

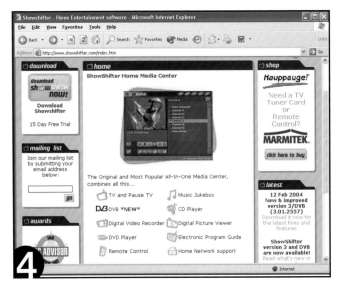

Check that you have an up-to-date driver for your TV tuner (or all-in-one graphics) card. This means a visit to the manufacturer's website. Also check that the card plays live TV with whatever software was supplied. You're then ready to download and install ShowShifter from **www.showshifter.com**. *At the time of writing the current version is 3.x, which is suitable for both analogue or digital (DVB) cards. The file size is 21MB so, unless you have a broadband connection, you can expect to wait up to two hours for it to download. On completion, there will be an executable file called ShowShifter-Setup.exe in your usual download folder.*

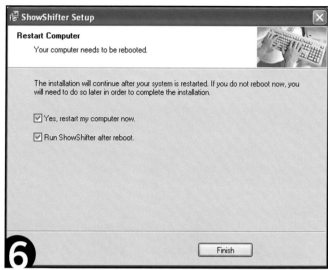

During installation ShowShifter will automatically check for updates, so make sure your internet connection is live before you start. Double click ShowShifter-Setup.exe to start the installation and respond to the various prompts throughout. The correct response is obvious in most cases but when you are asked to select an Electronic Programme Guide do not choose Titan TV. This is for the USA only. Instead, choose not to install a programme guide (we'll add one later).

On the final installation screen you must agree to a reboot before ShowShifter can be used. We also suggest that you leave Run ShowShifter after reboot checked. This will take you straight into the ShowShifter setup routine when your computer restarts.

If you did not set ShowShifter to start automatically, activate it by opening the ShowShifter group on the Start menu and clicking ShowShifter. You could also use ShowShifter in safe mode, which is a special reconfiguration mode in which settings can be changed at any time. Notice the question mark icon in the bottom left-hand corner of the opening screen. This invokes the help system if you need it, and is present on each setup screen. Click the right arrow to proceed.

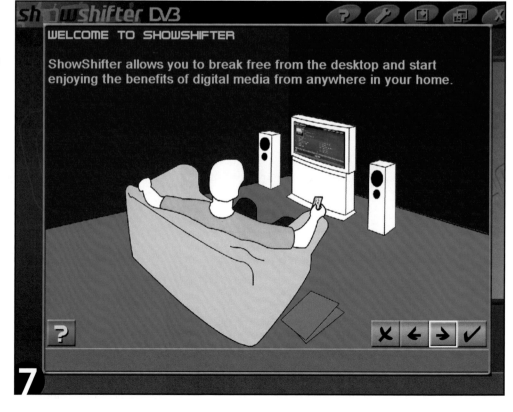

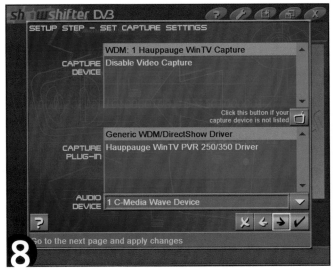

8

The next six screens are for information only. When you have viewed each one and clicked the right arrow each time, you will arrive at the first page of the setup wizard, shown here. On this screen you must choose a capture device (TV tuner), its driver (or 'capture plug-in') and an audio device (usually the internal sound card). In this example, the capture device is a Hauppauge WinTV capture card and the WDM designation indicates that it uses the Windows Driver Model (a system for making drivers work across a wide range of different Windows configurations). If a capture plug-in is listed with a name that indicates the exact model of your TV card, you might like to try it in preference to the WDM driver. It's really a question of suck it and see.

9

There is likely to be a delay of several seconds before the next screen appears, on which the country and TV standard will be correctly selected for you. If not, use the drop-down lists to change them. Tick either the Air or Cable box to indicate whether you receive your TV pictures by aerial or cable, and then click the right arrow to continue.

10

The selection you make in the Live Audio Line field specifies how your sound card receives live TV audio from the tuner card. This is likely to be via a connection to the sound card's line-in socket, but if this doesn't work satisfactorily you can try any of the other options on the drop-down list. The slider control is for audio volume when watching live TV (the setting for recorded TV can be adjusted on the next screen). The selection of a language is not necessary unless you are able to receive multilingual broadcasts. Click the right arrow.

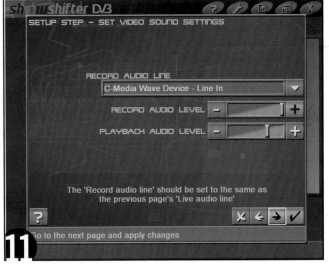

11

Your selection of Record Audio Line should be the same as the setting for the live TV audio line you chose in step 4. The slider control for Record Audio Level determines how loud recorded TV audio will be, and at this stage just leave it at maximum until you've had a chance to hear the results. Playback Audio Level determines the playback volume not only of recorded TV but of every Windows program that uses Wave output. This affects the playback of compressed music files, audio CDs and DVDs. Click the right arrow to continue.

Click the Start Autotune button in the bottom left-hand corner to search for channels. This is obligatory, even though you may have already set up channels using the software that came with your tuner card. Once all the channels have been found, click on each channel in turn to select it, and then click in the Channel Name section and use the keyboard to change the name. You'll probably need a printed programme guide to help you identify channels. Delete duplicate or unwanted channels by selecting them and clicking on the dustbin icon on the right. Note that in this example 17 channels have been found but they can't all be listed in the space available. Use the slider bar and arrows on the right to scroll.

Once you've named all the appropriate channels and deleted the remainder you'll probably want to change their order. To do this, select them one at a time and use the channel up-and-down arrows (in the toolbar on the extreme right of the screen) to move them up and down in the list. The composite video and S-Video channels may be useful to you if you ever need to connect your PC to a video camera or VCR/DVD player to access pre-recorded material. Click the right arrow to proceed to the final setup screen.

If you will be using your PC monitor to watch TV, select the 4:3 option. You should also select the 4:3 option if your computer has a TV-out socket and you will be connecting it to a standard, non-widescreen TV set. If you have a widescreen set, use the appropriate option for its screen type: plasma or non-plasma. Finally, click the tick mark in the bottom right-hand corner to complete the setup of ShowShifter and display the main menu.

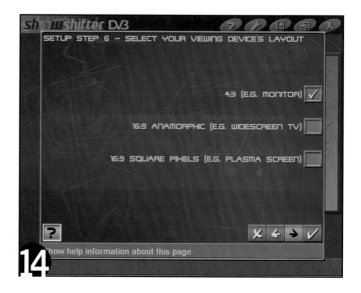

PART **5**

THE DIY ALTERNATIVE

Using ShowShifter

ShowShifter dramatically improves upon the software supplied with TV tuner cards. There's plenty to explore but here's a run-through of the basics. If you get stuck, visit the excellent discussion forums on the ShowShifter website (www.showshifter.com). Chances are you'll find somebody else has been in precisely the same pickle. If not, you can always post a message asking for help.

In the following steps overleaf, we look at the basic operation of ShowShifter in TV mode before moving on to install an EPG. ShowShifter's other modules are perfectly straightforward so get on top of this section first and the rest should be plain sailing.

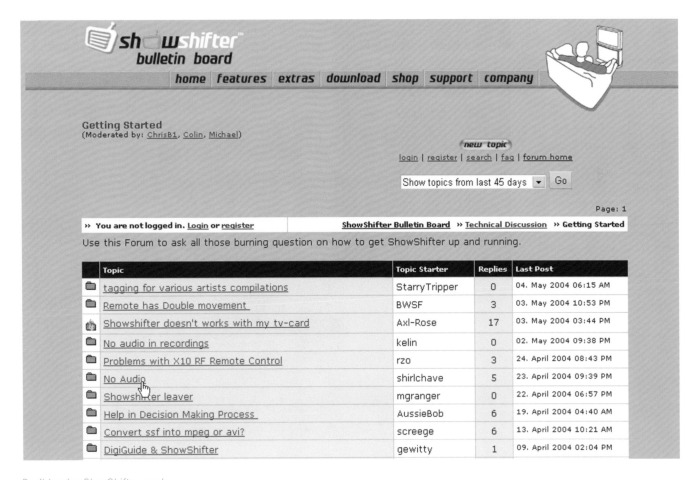

Don't be shy: ShowShifter can be tricky so seek advice in the online user forums.

137

This is the home screen and main menu of ShowShifter, with the major features running down the left-hand side and the most recently used TV programme or music visualisation playing in the main window. To switch to TV channel view, click on Television; or highlight it using the keyboard cursor up and down arrows and then press Enter.

From this screen every aspect of TV viewing, recording and time-shifting can be controlled. On the right is the display of the available channels you set up earlier, and just above the channel list are two tabs, marked TV and Files. Currently the Files tab is empty but here you will access your recordings in future. Beneath the preview window is the main TV control bar and below that is a second bar used for configuring TV reception and recording. To make your first recording, choose a channel and then click the Record button (a red circle) on the TV control bar.

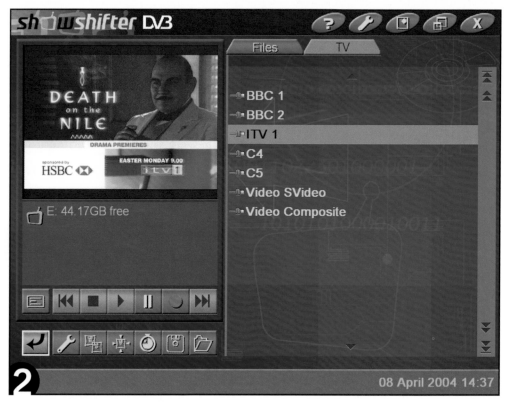

The display panel beneath the TV picture initially shows the length of the current recording in hours, minutes and seconds. After a short while, a second set of timings appears, indicating the maximum recording time. This depends on the free space on the hard disk drive and is just an estimate that is constantly adjusted according to the complexity of the video being saved. A percentage figure displayed after CPU tells you how hard your computer's processor is having to work to encode the video. If the figure is over 50%, it indicates that you'd be better off choosing a lower quality recording scheme that places less strain on the processor. To record for a preset period of time, click the record button repeatedly to cycle through options for 30, 60, 90, 120, 150, 180, 210 and 240 minutes, before eventually returning to unlimited recording. Click the Stop button (square icon) once you've recorded your first few minutes of video.

Click the Files tab to see the recording you've just made. It is identified by the day, time and date of its recording (and, when viewed in Windows Explorer, this is also its file name). To play the file, click on it. Click the TV tab to return to channel selection mode. Notice, however, that the recording continues to play, so to return to live TV viewing you must click the Stop button. In any event, live pictures will kick in automatically when the recorded video reaches its end.

A more sophisticated form of timed recording is possible using the timer page. To get here, click the stopwatch icon on the lower toolbar. Most of the options on this screen are self-evident, but before you start filling in the boxes you must click the Plus icon at the top right to create a new event. When you do so, a default half-hour recording starting immediately is pre-entered ready for editing. Give the event a descriptive name and change the start and end times accordingly. Also specify the correct channel for the recording and choose a repeat frequency if you want to record the same time slot more than once. The options are daily, weekly, Mon-Fri, Tue-Sat, weekends or never. We suggest setting up a test recording now to start in 5 or 10 minutes' time.

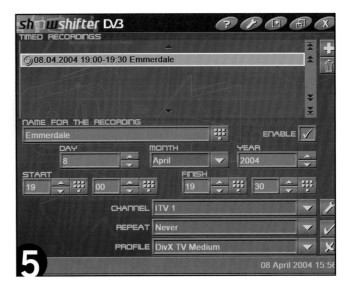

6 Finally select a profile to determine the quality of video to be recorded. The higher the quality, the more processing power is required, and the larger will be the resulting file. If your PC is up to it, the best choice is DivX TV Best. If you scroll down the list of options you'll see that there are alternative DivX Best modes for medium and fast processors, too. Return to TV mode, and wait for your timed recording to take place. During recording the TV display will switch automatically to the channel being recorded. It is not possible to watch a different channel while recording (just like Media Center).

7 Time-shifting is the ability to pause a live TV transmission and continue watching it later from the same point. When you click the Pause button, the program begins saving the live broadcast as a digital video file on the hard disk drive. When you press the Play button again to resume viewing after a break, what you actually see is the recording. As you watch this recorded material, ShowShifter continues to record the live broadcast so that you can continue to watch the programme to its end. To try this out, select a TV channel and then click on the Pause button (immediately to the left of the Record button). The picture on the screen will freeze and the display area below it will show the same elapsed time and time remaining figures as during normal recording. Try clicking Pause now and watch the frame freeze.

8 After two or three minutes of paused recording, click the Play button (to the left of Pause) and the picture will come back to life. You can see from the display beneath the picture that recording is still in progress, but the length of the recording remains constant because pre-recorded material is discarded as you watch it and newly recorded material takes its place. In this way the amount of recorded material always equals the duration of the original pause. If you click Pause again, you will see the length of recorded segment increase once more, continuing to do so as more video is added to the material carried over from the initial pause.

9 If you're not sure whether you will resume viewing a programme in the immediate future, press the Record button instead of Pause. You'll then be able to watch the permanent recording at a more convenient time. But you'll have to wait until the entire programme has been recorded.

Incidentally, if you find that the TV picture unexpectedly jumps from the preview window to full screen mode while you are perusing channels, don't be alarmed: this is by design. To return to channel view, simply click the right-hand mouse button. Alternatively, press Escape to go back to the ShowShifter home screen and select Television from there.

PART **5** The ShowShifter EPG

The Electronic Programme Guide (EPG) facility in ShowShifter is fiddly to set up but it does have the great advantage of being completely free to use. This is because it uses a system called XMLTV to scour web sites for free programme information and store it in a file using the XML format (an advanced form of the HTML language used to create standard web pages). Where things get messy is that the XMLTV program runs independently of ShowShifter, and you have to use a second program to pipe, or import, the XML data into ShowShifter before you can use it (by which point you may be sorely tempted to buy a Media Center . . . read on).

If all this sounds like too much hard work, consider a subscription to the DigiGuide service. If you download and install the DigiGuide software (there's a free 30-day trial) before you install ShowShifter, then ShowShifter detects it during installation. It then adds a plug-in that lets you right-click any programme in the guide and select Record program in ShowShifter without further complications. If you install DigiGuide after you've set up ShowShifter, however, this facility will not be available. The only way to force its activation is by reinstalling ShowShifter. See **www.digiguide.com** for details.

It's worth the trouble of setting up ShowShifter's Electronic Programme Guide because it offers more than just a convenient way of setting timer recordings. For example, every time you switch channels in full screen mode, the EPG delivers an onscreen display of what's currently showing and what's on next.

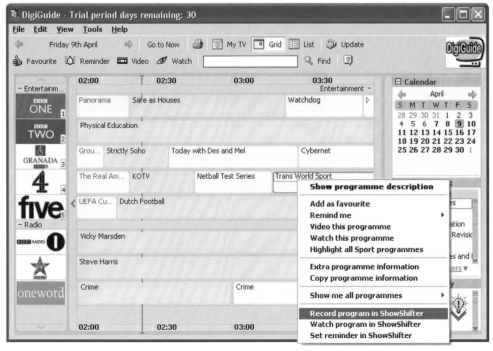

If working at the command-line level puts you off, a subscription to DigiGuide can make life very much easier.

Installing the EPG

One tip before we proceed: when typing instructions into command windows, it is essential to preserve the exact format of the examples given. An extra space here, a missing space there, or a hyphen instead of an underscore will cause your carefully typed commands to fail. When this happens, keep cool. Identify the error and then retype the entire command on a new line.

Download the XMLTV programs from **http://sourceforge.net/project/showfiles .php?group_id=39046**. *They come in the form of a single zipped file with the name xmltv-x.x.x-win32.zip, where the x.x.x is replaced by the current version number. For example, the version downloaded for this workshop was xmltv-0.5.31-win32.zip. Extract the files into the C:\Program Files folder, where they will be automatically installed in a folder with the same name as the zipped file. To simplify things for the following steps, open Windows Explorer and find this folder. Now right-click the folder, select Rename and call it EPG Tools.*

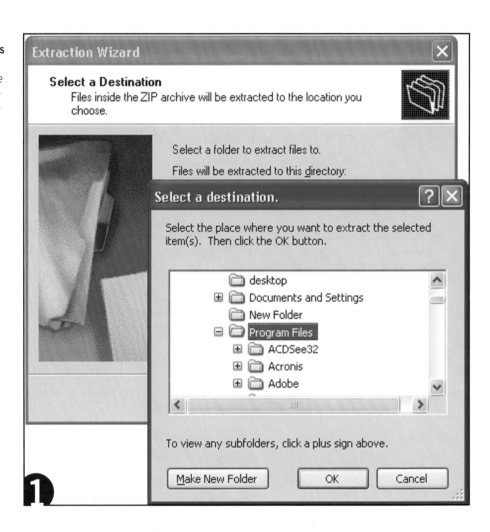

Make sure you are currently connected to the internet. Open a command window (in Windows XP you do this by clicking Start > All Programs > Accessories > Command Prompt) and then type this line:
cd \program files\epg tools
Press the Enter key to execute this command, and then follow it with:
xmltv.exe tv_grab_uk_rt --configure
When you press Enter to execute this command, the XMLTV program will find all the available television channels for the UK.

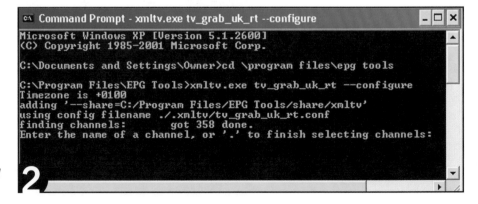

When all the available UK channels have been found, which takes a minute or more and occurs in the background, you need to select the channels for which listings are required. These will be the same ShowShifter channels you set up in step 12 on p136. Type BBC1 and press Enter for a list of BBC1 regional channels. Then press the number corresponding to your BBC region, followed by Enter. Repeat this process for each of the other ShowShifter channels. Note that BBC and ITV channels are typed without spaces; for C4 you must type 'Channel 4'; and for C5 the word 'Five'. When you have finished, press full stop followed by Enter to complete the process. Close the command window. You have now installed and configured XMLTV, and this does not need to be done again (praise be). From now on, whenever you need to run XMLTV you will start at step 4.

```
Command Prompt - xmltv.exe tv_grab_uk_rt --configure
Microsoft Windows XP [Version 5.1.2600]
(C) Copyright 1985-2001 Microsoft Corp.

C:\Documents and Settings\Owner>cd \program files\epg tools

C:\Program Files\EPG Tools>xmltv.exe tv_grab_uk_rt --configure
Timezone is +0100
adding '--share=C:/Program Files/EPG Tools/share/xmltv'
using config filename ./.xmltv/tv_grab_uk_rt.conf
finding channels:      got 358 done.
Enter the name of a channel, or '.' to finish selecting channels: BBC1
Which channel to add?
0: BBC1
1: BBC1 East
2: BBC1 London & SE
3: BBC1 Midlands
4: BBC1 North
5: BBC1 North East
6: BBC1 North West
7: BBC1 Northern Ireland
8: BBC1 Scotland
9: BBC1 South
10: BBC1 South West
11: BBC1 Wales
12: BBC1 West
13: None of the above are what I wanted
choose one: 3
Enter the name of a channel, or '.' to finish selecting channels: _
```

3

This step describes how to use XMLTV to grab channel listings for two days. You will need to be connected to the internet. Open a Command prompt window and then type the line:
cd \program files\epg tools
Press the Enter key to execute the above command, and then type:
xmltv.exe tv_grab_uk_rt --days 2 >listings.xml
followed by Enter.
The listings will be downloaded and stored in a file called Listings.xml in the EPG Tools folder. You may now close the command window. To grab listings for a longer period simply change the number of days in the command line, bearing in mind that the more days you specify, the longer the download.

```
Command Prompt
Microsoft Windows XP [Version 5.1.2600]
(C) Copyright 1985-2001 Microsoft Corp.

C:\Documents and Settings\Owner>cd \program files\epg tools

C:\Program Files\EPG Tools>xmltv.exe tv_grab_uk_rt --days 2 >listings.xml
Timezone is +0100
adding '--share=C:/Program Files/EPG Tools/share/xmltv'
using config filename ./.xmltv/tv_grab_uk_rt.conf
finding channels:      got 358 done.
getting dates for which listings available:      got 17 done.
getting 2 days of listings
time 20040409100000, channel Channel 4: ###############################
time 20040409100000, channel Five:      ########################
time 20040409100000, channel ITV1 Granada:      ##############################
time 20040409100000, channel BBC1 Midlands:      #######################
time 20040409100000, channel BBC2 Midlands:      ####################
time 20040410040000, channel Channel 4: ######
time 20040410040000, channel Five:      #####
time 20040410040000, channel ITV1 Granada:      ######
time 20040410040000, channel BBC1 Midlands:      ##
time 20040410040000, channel BBC2 Midlands:      #####
time 20040410060000, channel Channel 4: ###############################
time 20040410060000, channel Five:      ########################
time 20040410060000, channel ITV1 Granada:      #############################
time 20040410060000, channel BBC1 Midlands:      #############################
#
time 20040410060000, channel BBC2 Midlands:      ###########################
Accessed 18 web pages, downloaded 2006 Kb, duration 207 secs

C:\Program Files\EPG Tools>_
```

4

ShowShifter cannot use the data in the Listings.xml file until it is imported into ShowShifter's programme guide. This requires the help of a supplementary ShowShifter program with the snappy name of Hmnxmltv.exe. This can be downloaded by typing **http://www.inventv.com/download/hmn xmltv.zip** into your web browser (or by searching the support section of the ShowShifter website). It's a very small download of 122KB and it contains just three files. These should be unzipped and placed in the main ShowShifter folder. Unless you specified otherwise at the time of installation, this will be C:\ Program Files\Home Media Networks Limited\ShowShifter.

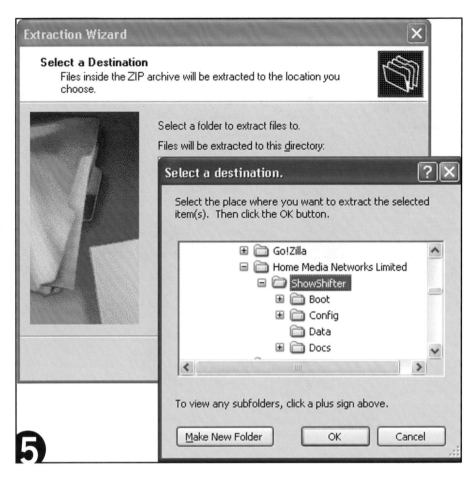

With the program safely installed, start Windows Explorer and navigate to the ShowShifter folder. Ensure that ShowShifter is not running at this point. Double click the Hmnxmltv.exe file to run it. It will look in vain in the ShowShifter folder for a Listings.xml file to import. To help it out use the Open file dialogue box to guide the program to the EPG Tools folder. Click OK, and the listings will be imported.

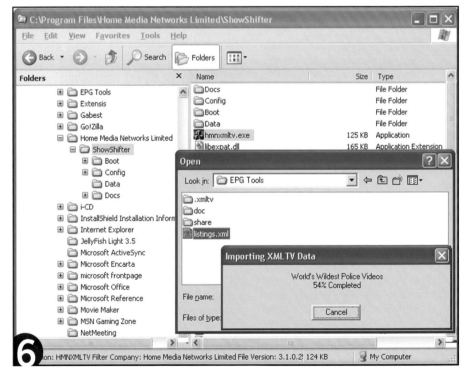

7 Start ShowShifter and select ShowGuide from the main menu. Click Grid View to check that the imported listings are in place. The single arrows at the top can be used to move forwards and backwards a few hours; the double arrows to move forwards and backwards by a full day; and the facing arrows to jump to the present time. The listings run from left to right in a timeline, with the leftmost listing representing the programme currently being broadcast. As a test, click on the current BBC1 show to select it.

8 This action displays a screen (not shown) on which you have five options: four are different ways of recording the show and the other is to watch the show now. When you click 'Watch this show' you'll be presented with the screen shown here, on which you need to select which of the pre-set channels corresponds to BBC1. It may seem obvious to you that BBC1 in the ShowGuide is represented by BBC1 in the pre-set channels, but remember that BBC1 is only a label you added yourself, and for all ShowShifter knows you might have called it Auntie or The Beeb. So select BBC1 and then click the tick in the bottom right-hand corner to map the programme guide channel to the ShowShifter channel and continue.

Press Escape to return to the ShowGuide programme grid and repeat the procedure for BBC2, and then for each of the other channels. As you do so, ShowGuide maps its pre-set channels to the ShowGuide and you will never have to go through this tedious procedure again. Incidentally, you can see in the screenshot how ShowGuide has adjusted the presentation of the programmes in the timeline to take account of the 25 minutes which have elapsed since Step 7.

An easier life?

Phew. Once you've downloaded XMLTV and Hmnxmltv and configured them for use with ShowShifter, the process of keeping programme listings up to date becomes much more straightforward. You run XMLTV once a week to gather the next 7-10 days' programmes and then use Hmnxmltv to read them into Showshifter. The downloading of software and its configuration, as described in the preceding steps, does not have to be repeated every time you want to refresh the programme guide.

If you fancy trying your hand at simple programming (involving only the typing of text files), it is possible to fully automate the Electronic Programme Guide by running XMLTV and Hmnxmltv from batch files that are executed at set times from within ShowShifter. There's no space to go into the process in detail here, but it is fully described in the Support section of the ShowShifter website.

Bottom line: ShowShifter is no Windows Media Center but it manages to offer similar features for a fraction of the price. We found it reasonably stable except when we tried to run other Windows programs at the same time, in which case it crashed or hung frequently. These unpredictable lock-ups can have a knock-on effect too, which you don't notice until the next time you try to update the Electronic Programme Guide. What happens is that when you try to import the XML programme listing into ShowShifter, you receive an error message to the effect that the EPG database cannot be opened. This stops you using the Electronic Programme Guide until such time as you reinstall ShowShifter and set up all the channels and channel names again. This is definitely a situation where prevention is better than cure.

The ideal scenario for ShowShifter, we reckon, is as a supplementary TV in a multi-TV household, or as the sole entertainment centre for an individual living in accommodation where space is limited. ShowShifter can turn an ordinary PC into a TV, digital video recorder and music centre for less than the price of a set of speakers, and that's no mean feat.

This error can stop you in your tracks and force you to reinstall ShowShifter from scratch.

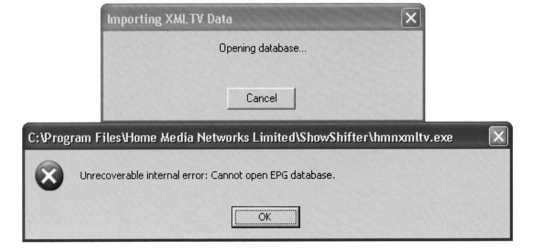

 PART **Using remote controllers**

The preceding step-by-step instructions are based on using the keyboard and mouse to operate ShowShifter, and there's no doubt that during the ShowShifter setup phase, when you're seated in front of your PC, this is definitely the easiest way to proceed. However, once everything is up and running, it must be easily operable from an armchair if you're really going to take ShowShifter seriously as a Media Center alternative.

Long-distance mouse

The remote control solution that involves the least fuss and expense is a radio-controlled mouse. They're cheap to buy, they work with all Windows programs, including ShowShifter, without any special configuration, and they don't trip people up. If the mouse follows the conventional design of two-buttons with a centre scroll wheel, then the left button is used to point and click at objects on the screen, the right button switches between full screen and menu modes, and the scroll wheel changes channels.

In any situation where ShowShifter requires alphanumeric input, such as when naming time-shifted video recordings, you can click the keypad icon (several tiny black squares arranged geometrically) and enter text by clicking individually on the table of alphanumeric characters.

You can get by with an on-screen keypad and a mouse in ShowShifter.

WinTV controllers

Several of the Hauppauge WinTV IR (infrared) tuners come bundled with remote controllers. Although not every button on these units has an equivalent ShowShifter function, there are more than enough active buttons to control every ShowShifter feature. Before you can use a Hauppauge Win TV remote you need to edit a file in the Windows folder called Irremote.ini. This is a text file and can be edited with Windows Notepad. The changes are described on the ShowShifter support page at **www.showshifter.com/support/hauppauge.htm**, from where you can cut and paste the changes into Irremote.ini.

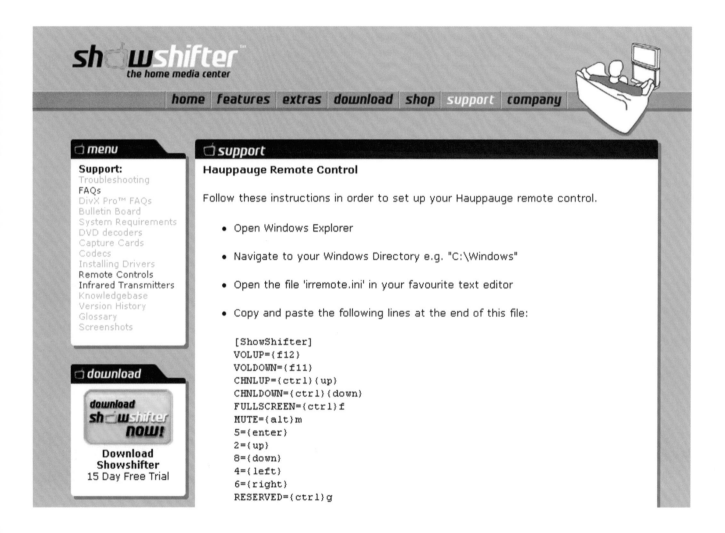

Having made the changes, use the Restart IR option in the Hauppauge group from the Windows Start > All Programs menu and you're ready to go. The cross-shaped arrangement of the 2, 4, 6 and 8 buttons on the remote becomes a virtual four-way directional controller, with the 5 button at the centre of the keypad acting as an Enter or Confirm key. The button marked 'Reserved' switches between full screen and menu modes. Other Hauppauge keys for channel changing and volume control continue to work as usual.

Copy and paste this code rather than attempt to type it directly.

Generic IR controllers

Almost any IR controller designed for Windows can be used with ShowShifter provided it has six buttons (four for direction, one for menu/full screen and one for Enter). If it has a seventh button to act as Cancel/Escape, this is even better. To assign the buttons on the remote controller to the appropriate functions in ShowShifter, start ShowShifter and click the spanner icon on the opening screen to view the main settings page. Click IR Trainer, and on the next page click Start IR Trainer. Follow the onscreen instructions. These lead you to the training page, shown here, where actions can be assigned to specific buttons on the remote unit.

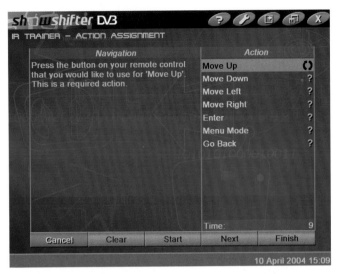

Training a generic Windows remote to control ShowShifter.

Marmitek PC Control unit

Marmitek's PC Control is the ultimate remote controller, suitable not only for ShowShifter and general PC usage but also configurable for any other remotely controlled domestic devices (you can see one on p132). It transmits to a USB wireless receiver connected to your PC and also sends an IR beam if you want to control other equipment. It works straight out of the box with ShowShifter provided you first run the X10 RFAnywhere program (this can be found in the ShowShifter program group in the Start > All Programs menu).

The two big advantages of the Marmitek unit are that it does not require a line-of-sight connection to its receiver unit and that it is blessed with every conceivable button you might require to operate the non-TV features of ShowShifter, such as DVD and audio CD playback. It also has dedicated buttons for TV recording, time-shifting, pause, mute and all other ShowShifter functions. Its only real flaw is that it lacks alphabetic keys, so you are still forced to use the onscreen keypad when you wish to enter text. This isn't a problem when ShowShifter is able to automatically identify an audio CD using the FreeDB internet database, as seen here, but it's not much fun entering track details for unknown CDs via the onscreen keypad.

If you fancy a remote that requires minimal configuration, check out a Marmitek PC Control (this can be ordered through the ShowShifter store). Here we're using it to control ShowShifter's CD module.

6

PART 6

Appendices

Appendix 1
Making DVDs in Media Center

When you record TV programmes with Media Center, they are stored as digital video files on the hard disk drive in a specific folder. Its full path is: C:\Documents and Settings\All Users\Documents\Recorded TV. An easier way to get to it is to open the Shared Documents folder from any Windows Explorer window and look for the Recorded TV sub-folder.

As we've said, Media Center uses a proprietary file developed by Microsoft. It is essentially the MPEG-2 file format used in the creation of DVD Movies, but with an added 'wrapper' that enables content to be copy-protected. The idea is to stop you recording the latest series of *The Simpsons*, burning it to DVD and flogging copies down at the local car boot sale. That's fine, but will only have a point when television suppliers start incorporating Digital Rights Management (DRM) encoding in their broadcasts. This has yet to be seen on any large scale.

For now, it leaves you with a blunt file format problem that makes it tricky to archive recordings to DVD. The problem is simply this: most video editing and DVD authoring programmes don't recognise and can't work with DVR-MS files. Even Windows Movie Maker 2, which is supplied with Windows XP (and thus every Media Center), baulks at DVR-MS files. This means that you can't simply grab a recorded programme file from your Recorded TV folder and edit it or burn it directly to disc. How, then, to keep precious recordings when disk space runs tight?

The Recorded TV folder. Note the huge file sizes: these video recordings are between 1 and 4GB each.

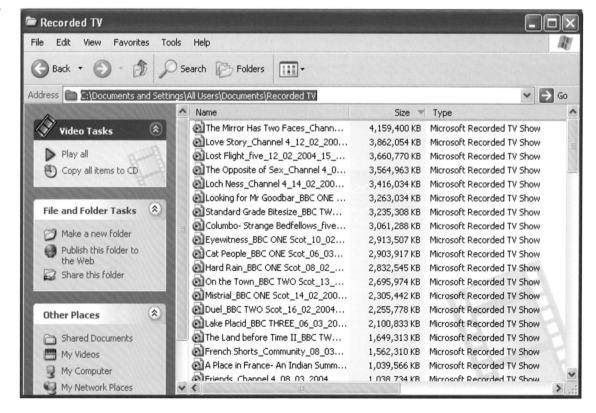

Workarounds

It's perfectly possible to burn a DVR-MS recording to a blank recordable DVD or CD disc as a simple data file. This at least gives you a backup copy of favourite shows or films. You could then play this file with the Windows Media Player program in the Windows XP environment directly from the disc. Indeed, you could even copy the file back to the Recorded TV folder when you have sufficient free disk space, whereupon Media Center will list and play it like any other recording.

You can also play DVR-MS files on any other Windows XP computer – not just your Media Center – so long as it has had a specific Windows update installed. Full details can be found at: **http://support.microsoft.com/default.aspx?scid=kb;EN-US;810243**.

Again, though, this doesn't address the issue of wanting to make a DVD movie that can be played in any DVD player (as opposed to a computer's DVD drive).

Help is at hand. Sonic PrimeTime is a software application that ties in rather nicely with Media Center and does, in fact, let you burn DVR-MS files directly to DVD in the standard movie format i.e. it makes discs that your granny can play in her DVD player. Indeed, once installed, it even adds a new Create DVD option to the main Media Center menu.

When you select Create DVD, PrimeTime launches in a Media Center-style interface (not within Media Center itself, unfortunately) and automatically finds all recorded programmes in your Recorded TV folder. It can also be controlled entirely with the remote. Pop a blank recordable DVD disc in your writer drive (assuming your Media Center has one), select one or more recordings, and choose Burn DVD. Some time later – it can take hours – you'll end up with a 'proper' DVD movie of your chosen programmes or films, replete with a title page. If you don't have a DVD writer, you can create lower-quality Video CDs i.e. DVD-style movies on recordable CD media.

We expect to see many similar approaches from other software developers, but at the time of writing PrimeTime is the best bet. If you can handle a 65MB download (3 hours over a modem; about 20 minutes over a 512Kbps broadband connection), experiment with the free trial version. You'll find this at: **www.sonic.com**.

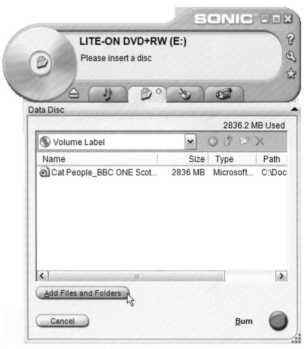

If you try to import a DVR-MS file into a standard video editing program like Movie Maker, this is what you will see.

It's easy to save DVR-MS files directly to disc, but don't confuse this with making a DVD movie. Data discs don't play in DVD players.

DVR-MS playback capability in Windows XP comes courtesy of an update.

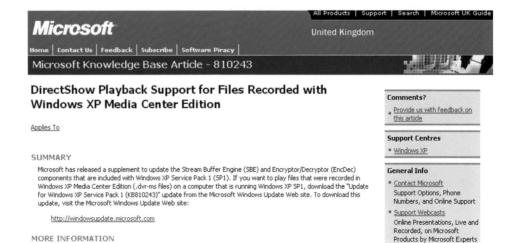

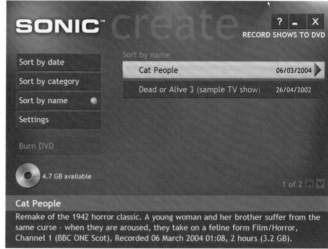

If only Media Center came with this menu option as standard. One day, we believe, it will.

Pick a programme and PrimeTime will make a movie.

Cut!

For all its welcome integration with Media Center and native support for DVR-MS files, PrimeTime doesn't let you edit your recordings before committing them to disc. If this is an issue for you – you might want to remove the adverts, for instance – then look for one of the rare but growing band of video editing applications that can convert DVR-MS to standard MPEG-2. Again, a Sonic program, MyDVD, can do this, albeit at a fairly rudimentary level. It even has a welcome Get Recorded TV Shows button on the main interface. Download the 150MB(!) trial version from the Sonic website.

Alternatively, try one of the utilities available on The Green Button website (**www.thegreenbutton.com**). For example, a program called DVR Ripper promises to convert DVR-MS files to MPEG-2 for free, although it does require that other software from a different developer is pre-installed first. Be sure to study the ReadMe file if you download such utilities, and perhaps conduct a quick internet search to see what success others have had with it.

In summary, then, playing recorded TV shows is not a problem. You can do this from within Media Center itself (obviously) or on any other Windows XP computer subject to the proviso about the update stated above. You can easily make backup copies on recordable CD or DVD discs, but these can't be played in standard DVD players. However, there are applications out there that let you both burn recorded shows to disc in DVD movie format and, optionally, edit them first.

Do these programs always work or always work smoothly? No, in our experience, they do not, which is why we heartily recommend playing around with the fully-featured trial versions before shelling out.

Click Get Recorded TV Shows and Sonic MyDVD goes straight to the Recorded TV folder. DVR-MS files are welcome.

The Green Button is a great resource for all Media Center related matters.

PART ⑥ **Appendix 2
ID3 tags and Windows
Media Player**

An ID3 tag is a snippet of text-only information bundled semi-invisibly with your MP3 and WMA music files. It contains information about the track – the artist, track title and number, album, year, genre and so forth – and can be read and displayed both by hardware and software MP3 players. If you have a portable player that displays track information during playback, for instance, that information is being read from the ID3 tag. Similarly with Windows Media Player and, by extension, Media Center: on-screen information in the My Music module comes from these tags.

The trouble is that ID3 tags can be wrong. This is particularly true when you download tracks through file-sharing networks, particularly the illegal ones. Tags may be incomplete, misleading or just plain missing. Because tags are all that Media Center has to go on – file names and folder hierarchies are irrelevant in this context – this accounts for why your music collection may very well not show up as you would like it to in My Music. The slightest inconsistency can throw it off track, as we saw with the examples of artist name misspellings on p105. The way around it is to fine-tune your tags. You can do this in a number of ways.

Tweaking tags

You can view any track's ID3 tag very easily in Windows. Right-click the file, select Properties, open the Summary tab, and click Advanced. Here you will see the ID3 information. In fact, you can double-click any field and edit the tag directly, either to fill in the blanks or to correct mistakes.

Windows lets you check and edit ID3 tags on a file-by-file basis. If you have a year to kill, this would be a good strategy for tag management.

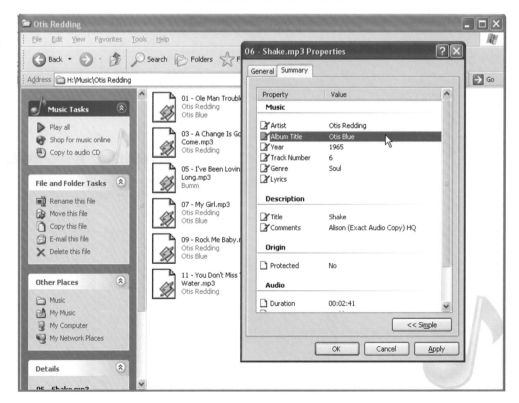

Most MP3 software players also let you edit tags. The ever-popular Winamp, for instance, is easy to use. During playback, right-click any track in the Playlist window, select File Info, and edit away.

It's an awfully slow way to proceed, though. To speed things up, try one of the specialist ID3 tag tools. MP3-TagIt, for instance, is a shareware (free to try) program that can search selected folders and present the totality of tag information in one editable screen. It lets you upgrade version 1 tags to version 2, and the Bulk Edit button affords a quick way to change ID3 field details for a whole bunch of tracks simultaneously. Get it from **http://plastiekske.tripod.com/index1.html**.

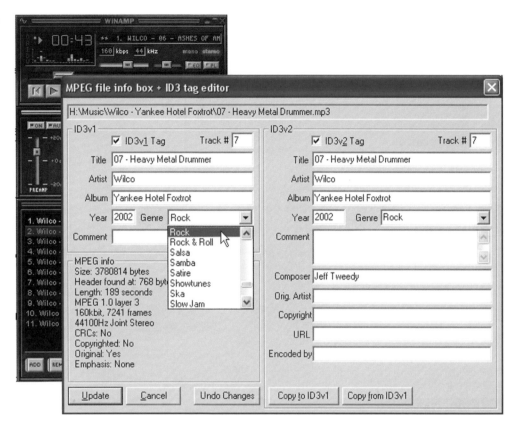

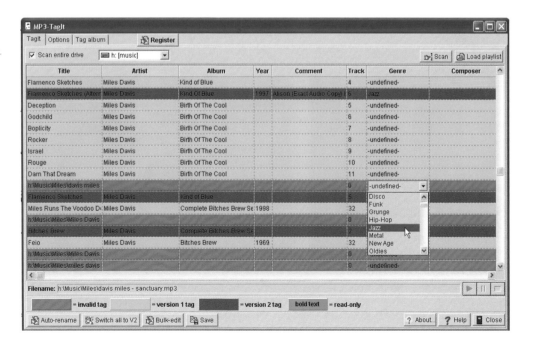

Editing ID3 tags in Windows Media Player

As you would expect, Windows Media Player also lets you modify ID3 tags. It also comes with some pretty powerful batch editing features. Here we'll modify the ID3 tag details for three albums that have been wrongly accredited to Gillian Welsh rather than Welch.

Open the Media Library in Windows Media Player and browse your music collection. We have selected Gillian Welsh in the artist view. By clicking the little plus icon to the left of an artist's name, you can see each album by that artist (if indeed you have more than one). If you now click on one of the albums, you'll see its tracks listed in the upper window pane to the left. Or if you click on the artist's name, you'll see each and every track by that artist, as shown here. As these are all wrongly attributed to the mythical Ms Welsh, we want to change the lot in one hit.

Click on the first track in the list, hold down the Shift key on your keyboard, and click the last track. This selects every track in the list. Alternatively, you could select a number of individual tracks by holding down the Control key while you click on each in turn. Now right-click any one of the selected tracks and choose Advanced Tag Editor from the popup menu.

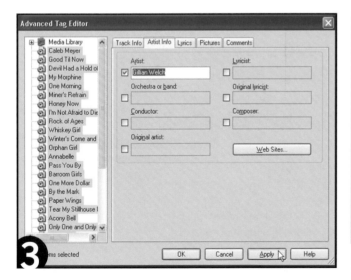

Open the Artist Info tab and put a tick in the box next to the Artist field. This makes that particular field editable. Now make your change. Here, we are changing the artist's name from Welsh to Welch. Click Apply and then OK. Back in the Media Library view, the change is immediate: the artist is now displayed as Gillian Welch and each track is now correctly attributed.

In this screenshot, we have selected All Music in the Media Library to see a complete track list (all 4,876 of them). If you right-click the column headers, you can determine which ID3 tags are shown and which are hidden. You can also then click on any column header to sort tracks by that category. Click the Genre header, for instance, to group your entire music collection by genre rather than by track title, artist name or any other criteria. It's a handy way of checking the extent of your Trip Hop collection.

Note too that Windows Media Player includes a column that isn't actually part of the ID3 format data, namely star ratings. We saw these ratings in Media Center earlier (p.105). To change a rating, point at the (default) three star rating next to any track and click on the one, two, four or five star option when it pops up. Repeat as often as you like. In this way, Media Center will be able to compile an auto-playlist based on your favourite tracks.

In one of its smartest features, Windows Media Player can update ID3 information automatically from an internet database and throw in album covers, reviews and web links, too. To see this in action, make sure your PC has an open internet connection and select any album in the Media Library. If data is already available, you should see the album cover plus a track list in the lower pane to the left. If not, right-click the album title and select Find Album Info. This instructs Windows Media Player to scurry off to the database and retrieve likely-looking hits.

In this example, it returned several possibilities and displayed them in the lower window on the right (only one can be seen without scrolling). The trick here is matching the precise album version with the correct track details. The track currently selected in the top pane is entitled 'Honey Now', and Windows Media Player suggests that this is, or might be, track 7 on a 1998 album called 'Hell among the Yearlings' (the track's ID3 tag currently contains no track number or year data). This is spot on, so we can click on the album cover image to confirm the choice.

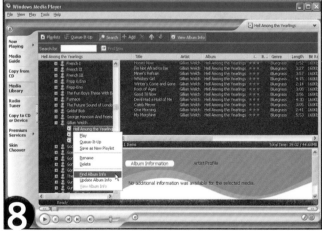

The ID3 tag is automatically amended accordingly. Incidentally, note that this track's ID3 tag now says that it belongs to the Folk genre, not Bluegrass (ID3 tags should never be taken as gospel). Windows Media Player has now selected the second track in the list and suggests that it's called 'I'm Not Afraid to Die' from the same album. Again, we can click on this to confirm it and move on down through the list.

9

The updated information should be reflected in Media Center next time you open My Music, although it can take a while for it to catch up with changes. Here we can see the album we just modified, now adorned with an album cover and correctly attributed to Gillian Welch.

10

Where an album or a track is completely lacking in ID3 data, Windows Media Player has nothing to go on and will return a blank when you ask it to Find Album Info (as in Step 6) . You might now opt to enter ID3 information manually on a track-by-track basis with the Advanced Tag Editor. Alternatively, click the Edit track information option in the lower pane. This generates a handy ID3 form for quick data entry.

11

You can also try giving Windows Media Player a clue or two about the music. Select the Refine your search option, select a track, and fill in what you can about the title, artist and album. The file name may or may not be helpful. Here, it is certainly not: for some reason, the track is called 'Questions' but the song is unmistakably Sinatra's rendition of 'All The Way'. Click the Search button and let the program work its magic.

12

Sometimes this works and sometimes it doesn't. Here, luckily, it did. Windows Media Player returned the correct album details, identified the song and suggested that it should be track number 15. Don't be fooled into thinking that the software 'listens' to the music or recognises it in any way, mind: this is all merely a matter of matching ID3 or other data to a database. We can now click the details to accept them and repeat the procedure for the next track. Or . . .

It would be quicker to simultaneously select all the remaining tracks in this album and use the Advanced Tag Editor to update the artist, album, genre and year ID3 information for all tracks simultaneously, just as in Steps 2 and 3. Be sure not to enter anything in the Track title field or else all tracks will end up with the same name. All that remains now is to edit the track title field for each track individually.

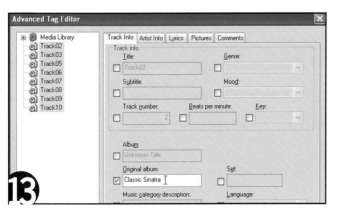

13

Working with playlists

If ID3 tags contain information about track numbers, Windows Media Player and Media Center will play an album's tracks in the correct order unless you specifically ask it to shuffle things about. This means that you don't necessarily have to create a playlist per album. However, it's useful to be able to group tracks from unrelated albums (or folders, if stored on different drives or devices) and hear them played together.

Click the Playlist button in Windows Media Player and select New Playlist. In the Playlist Name field, call it something memorable. We've gone for 'Easy Listening'. You can now sort your music collection in the left window by album, artist, genre or however else you fancy, and browse for tracks that you want to include in the playlist.

Click a track in the left window and it automatically gets added to the playlist on the right. Continue for as long as you like. To customise the playlist running order, select any track in the playlist and use the up and down arrows to reposition it. Click OK when you're done.

Your new playlist is now accessible from the My Playlists menu in the Media Library and can be played or edited from there. To remove a track, right-click it and select Delete from Playlist. Also, at any time in the future, you can add new tracks to this or any other playlist: just right-click the track, select Add to Playlist from the popup menu, and select the appropriate playlist from the proffered suggestions.

More importantly, perhaps, your playlist is now playable from within Media Center. From the main My Music menu, select Playlists, then My Playlists, and scroll through until you find the name you gave it in Step 1. You can play or shuffle tracks here – by default, they will play in the order you left them in Step 2 – but not, unfortunately, edit the playlist. For that, it's back to Windows Media Player.

Working with CDs

Windows Media Player also attempts to identify audio CDs in much the same way as it works with MP3 and WMA files. When it stumbles, as it certainly will with home-recorded compilations, you can help it along.

It is particularly useful doing this in Windows Media Player before you copy an unrecognised CD with Media Center. Once you tell Windows Media Player what's on a disc, it remembers this information and recognises the CD next time you pop it in the drive. Because Windows Media Player and My Music are so closely related (one and the same, in fact), this means that the CD shows up with correct album, artist and track data in Media Center and can be copied with this information intact.

Pop your CD into the drive when Windows Media Player is running, or allow the program to auto-play the disc. Click on Now Playing in the Media Library section. Now right-click any track and select Find Album Info.

When the programme fails, it offers a couple of refined search options where you can enter artist or album information, just as in Steps 11 and 12 above. This may help with obscure commercial recordings. However, if you made the disc yourself, select the third option. Click Next. This opens up an ID3-style database where you can give your 'album' a title and complete individual track information. Work your way through them all.

When you play this CD in Media Center's My Music module, the information you just entered will be available on-screen during playback. If you then choose to copy the CD, it will be transposed as ID3 tags on a track-by-track basis.

PART ⑥ Appendix 3
Glossary

AGP	Accelerated Graphics Port. A motherboard interface used exclusively by 3D video cards.
ASF	Advanced Systems Format. A file format used for video files.
AVI	Audio Video Interleaved. A file format used for video files.
BMP	Bitmap. A file format used for digital images.
CD	Compact Disc. An optical (i.e. read by laser) storage medium commonly used to distribute audio (music CDs) and data (CD-ROMs).
CD-R/-RW	CD-Recordable and CD-Rewriteable. The two recording formats used to record (write) blank CDs in computer drives.
CD-ROM	CD-Read Only Memory. A CD-ROM can be read in a computer drive but not recorded (written) to. Most software is distributed on CD-ROM.
Composite video	A standard used to feed video signals from one device to another. TV tuner cards often use the composite video interface to send images to televisions sets.
CPU	Central Processing Unit. A computer's processor.
CRT	Cathode Ray Tube. A glass tube used to produce the on-screen images in most television sets and older computer monitors.
DAB	Digital Audio Broadcasting. Radio stations transmitted as a high-quality digital signal.
DirectX	Microsoft software that allows third-party programs to interact seamlessly with Windows.
DivX	A compression codec for digital video that preserves quality without resulting in massive file sizes.
DRM	Digital Rights Management. Generic name for technologies that (seek to) prevent copyright material from being copied and distributed without permission.

DTT	Digital Terrestrial Television. Television channels transmitted digitally but with reception via a rooftop aerial rather than a cable or satellite service.
DVB-T	Digital Video Broadcast. See DTT.
DVD	Digital Versatile (or Video) Disc. A high-capacity optical (i.e. read by laser) storage medium, particularly popular for distributing movies.
DVI	Digital Visual Interface. A connectivity standard used for connecting digital monitors to computers. DVI is the successor to analogue-only VGA.
DVR-MS	Microsoft's proprietary file format used by Media Center to record video (television shows). DVR-MS files can incorporate DRM copy-protection technology.
EPG	Electronic Programme Guide. Detailed TV listings that you can use on a computer, usually downloaded from the internet.
Ethernet	A standard for joining computers in a network.
FM	Frequency Modulation. An analogue radio technology.
GB	Gigabyte. A measure of storage capacity, particularly on hard disk drives. One Gigabyte equals 1,024 Megabytes.
GHz	Gigahertz. A measure of how fast a processor can work. One Gigahertz equals one billion cycles per second.
GIF	Graphic Interchange Format. A file format used for digital images, restricted to 256 colours.
HTML	Hypertext Mark-up Language. A coding language used mainly to design and produce web pages.
IEEE 1394	A very fast digital interface particularly suited to connecting digital camcorders to computers. also known as FireWire (an Apple trademark).
IEEE 802.11a/b/g	Wireless networking standards. For home use, 'b' is the most common but is now being

	superseded by the faster 'g' and 'a' versions.		picked up with a rooftop aerial.
IR	Infrared. A light-wave technology commonly used by remote controls and receivers to communicate without wires.	SCART	An interface commonly used to connect a TV with audio-visual devices like VCRs and STBs.
JPG (or JPEG)	Joint Photographic Experts Group. A file format used for digital images. JPG offers high but lossy (data is discarded) compression that results in small file sizes.	SPDIF	Sony/Philips Digital Interface. Standards for transmitting a digital audio signal. The connections can be electrical (plugs and sockets) or optical (fibre-optic cables that transmit the signal with light).
Kbps	Kilobits per second. A measure of the speed of data transfer.	STB	Set-top box. A generic name for a device that receives and decodes a television signal: satellite, cable or DTT/DVB-T.
LCD	Liquid Crystal Display. A technology used to create slim, lightweight and flat-screen monitors (and occasionally TVs).	S-Video	A higher-quality alternative to composite video, also common on TV tuner cards.
LED	Light Emitting Diode. A light that, in computer terms, usually indicates live power or some kind of activity.	TFT	Thin Film Transistor. A high-quality display technology used with LCD screens.
MB	Megabyte. A measure of storage capacity. A floppy disk holds just 1.44MB.	TIF (or TIFF)	Tagged Image (File) Format. A file format used for digital images. In contrast to JPG, the TIF format offers non-lossy compression (no data is discarded) to produce smaller files.
MP3	Motion Pictures Expert Group Audio Layer-3. A file format used for digital music. An MP3 file allows high-quality audio to be highly compressed without significant loss of quality.	USB	Universal Serial Bus. An interface used to connect peripheral devices to computers. The fast USB 2 version is now the norm.
MPEG-1/2	File formats used for digital video. MPEG-2 offers higher picture quality than MPEG-1 and is used in the creation of commercial DVD movies.	VCR	Video Cassette Recorder. A device used for playing pre-recorded video tapes and for recording TV to tape.
PCI	Peripheral Component Interconnect. An expansion slot used on computer motherboards, ideal for internal accessories like TV tuners.	VGA	Video Graphics Array. The basic standard governing a video card's output and the corresponding display. The term is often used to refer to the monitor interface on a video card. This is an analogue interface, in contrast to DVI, which is the digital equivalent.
PVR	Personal Video Recorder. A generic name given to any device that offers advanced video-recording features like time-shifting (pausing live TV) and one-click series recording. PVRs usually use a hard disk for video storage and rely upon an Electronic Programme Guide.	VHS	Video Home System. The recording system used to record video on magnetic tapes that can be played in a VCR.
RAM	Random Access Memory. A computer's dynamic 'working space' memory, as opposed to long-term storage memory like a hard disk drive.	Wi-Fi	Wireless Fidelity. A generic term given to the IEEE 802.11 wireless network technologies.
		WMA	Windows Media Audio. A Microsoft file format used for sound files.
RF	Radio Frequency. Radio technology used to broadcast television channels which can be	WMV	Windows Media Video. A Microsoft file format used for video files.

Index

ACKNOWLEDGEMENTS

The author and publisher would like to thank the following companies for their help in the preparation of this manual:

Scott Colvey
Paul Wardley
Evesham Technology – www.evesham.com
Packard Bell – www.packardbell.co.uk
Shuttle – www.shuttle.com
Hauppauge Digital Europe – www.hauppauge.co.uk
Home Media Networks – www.showshifter.com

Author	**Kyle MacRae**
Copy Editor	**Shena Deuchars**
Photography	**Iain McLean**
Front cover photo	**Simon Clay**
Design	**Simon Larkin**
Page build	**Chris Fayers**
Index	**Nigel d'Auvergne**
Project Manager	**Louise McIntyre**